# COLORING BOOK

## EASTER EGG

+40 Coloring Pages

By bookidos
Designed in Barcelona 2020

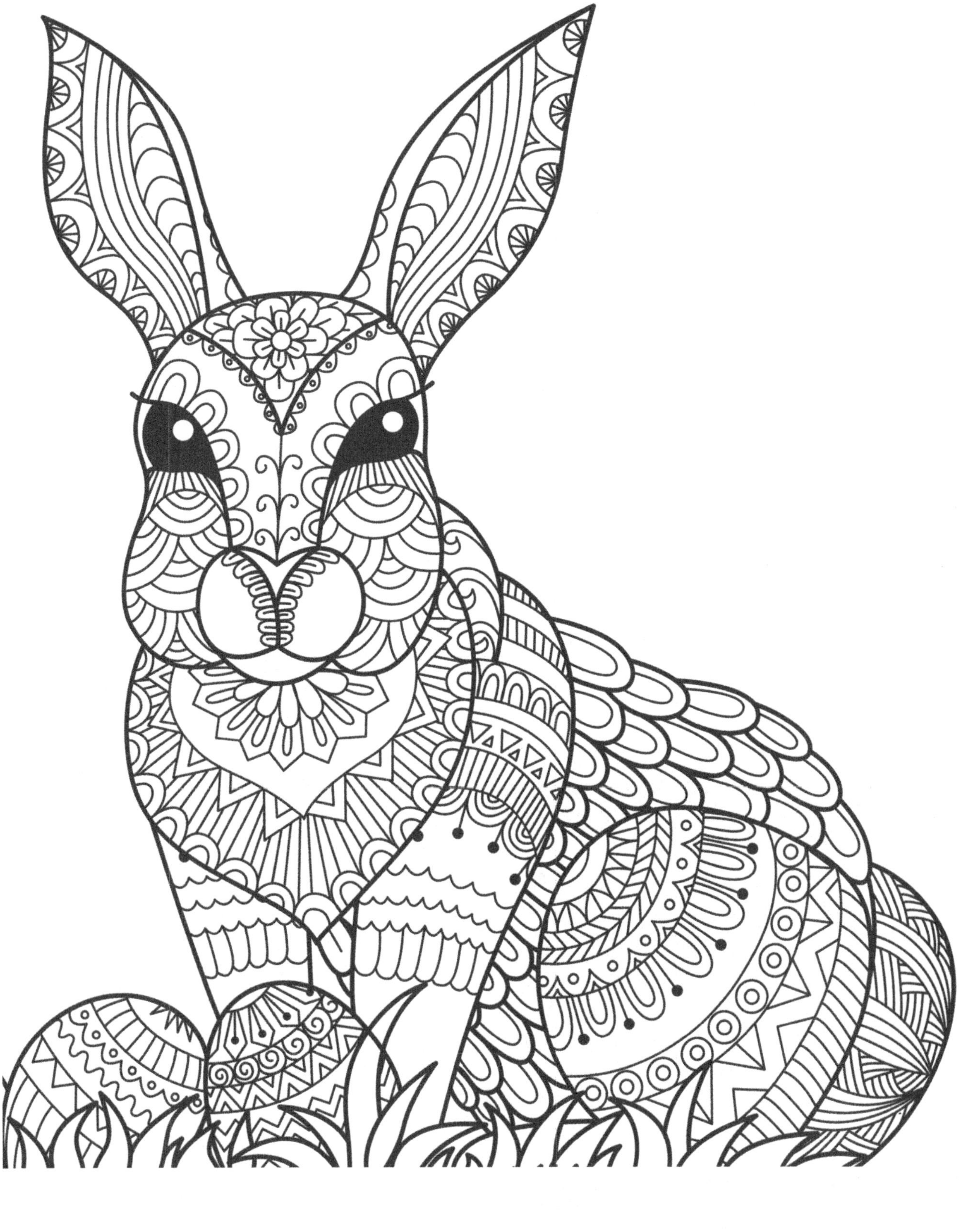

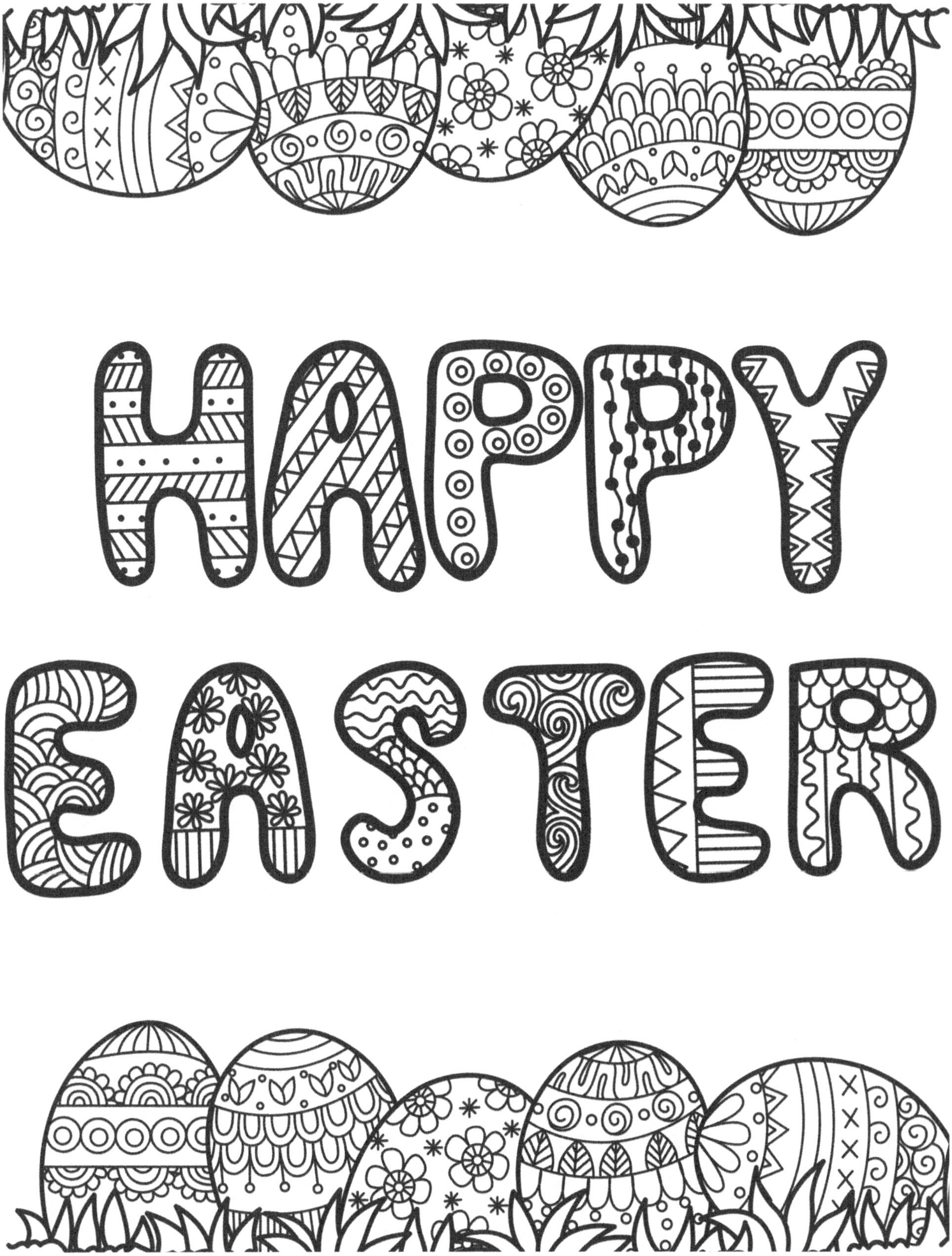
HAPPY
EASTER

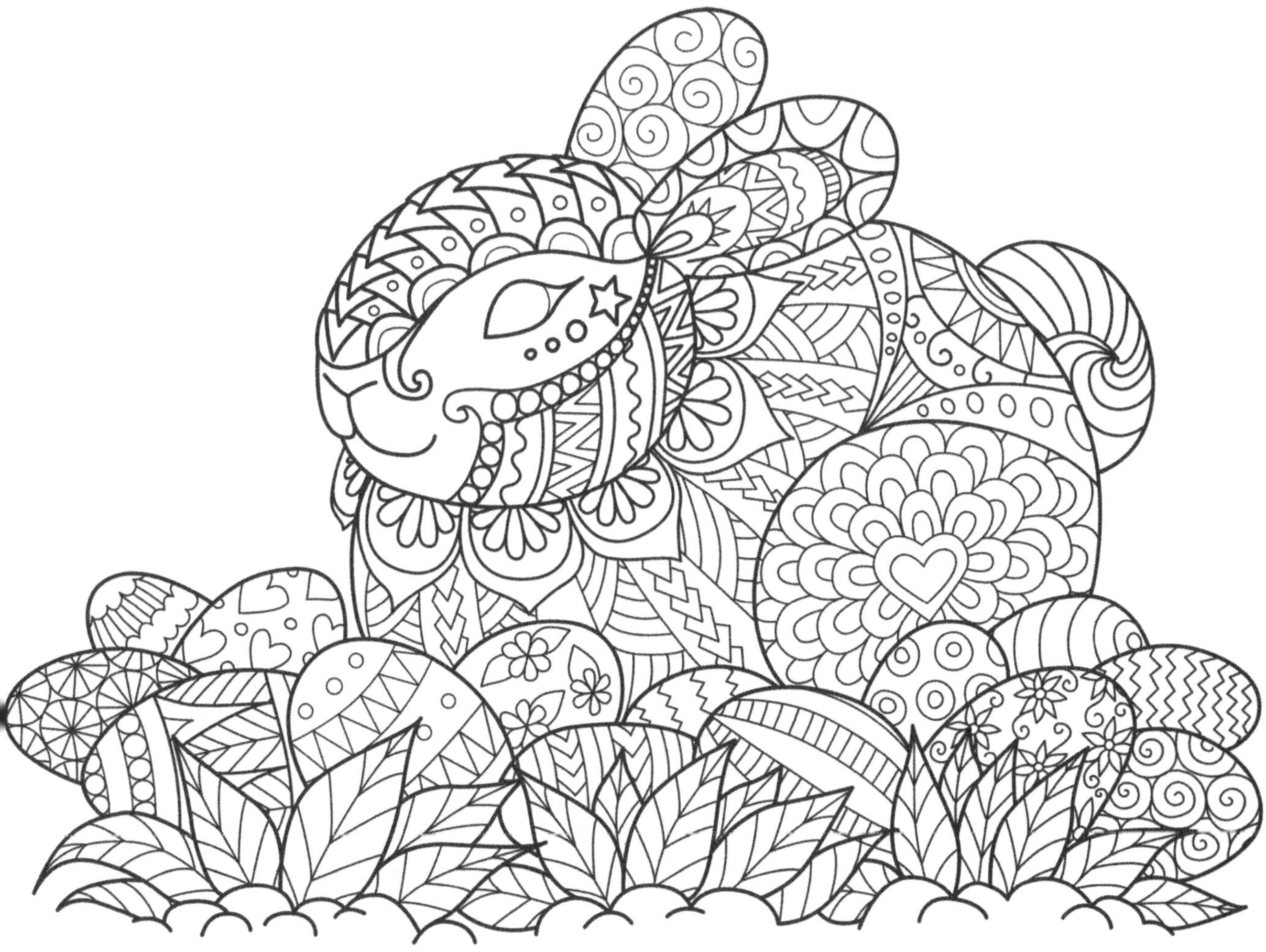

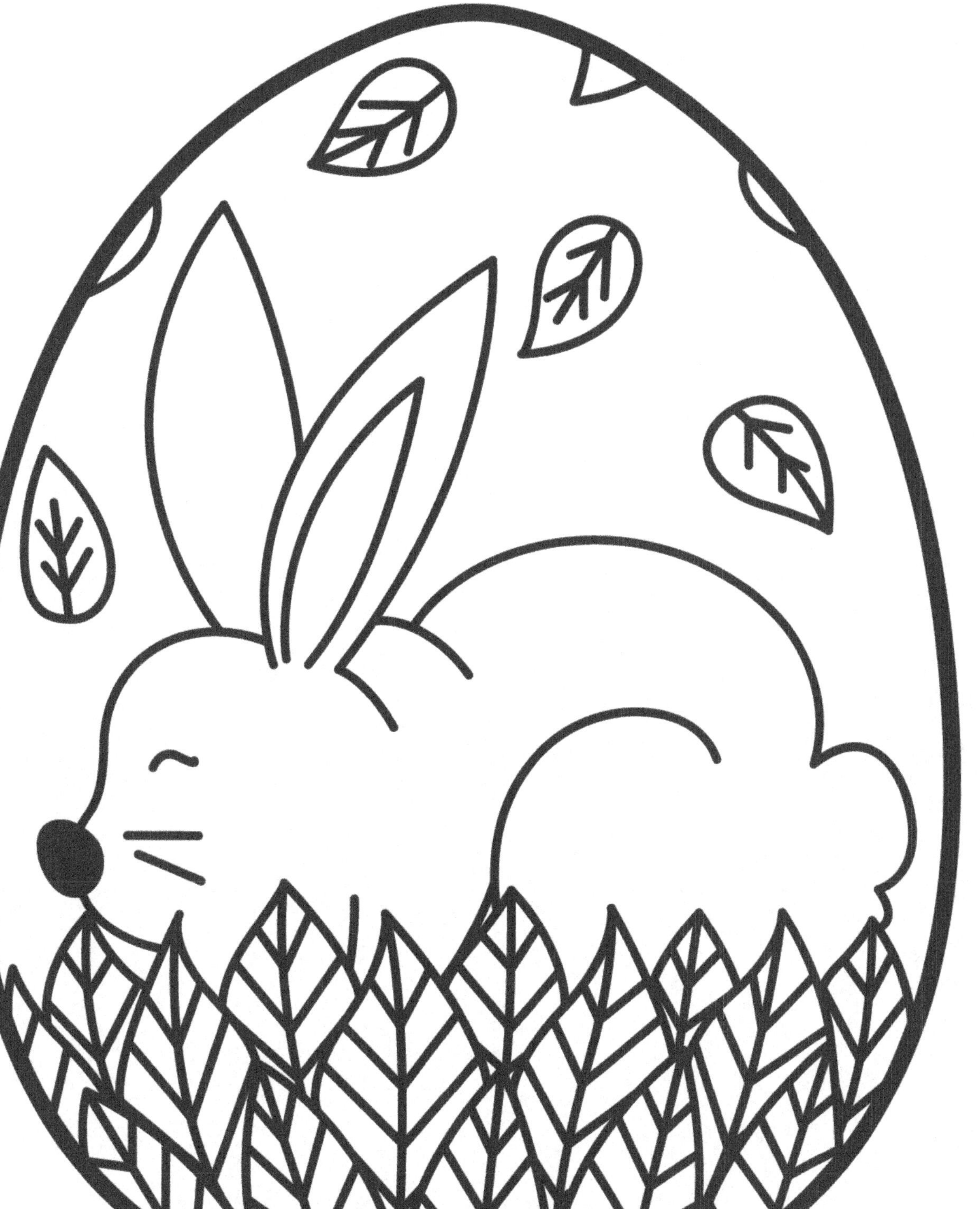

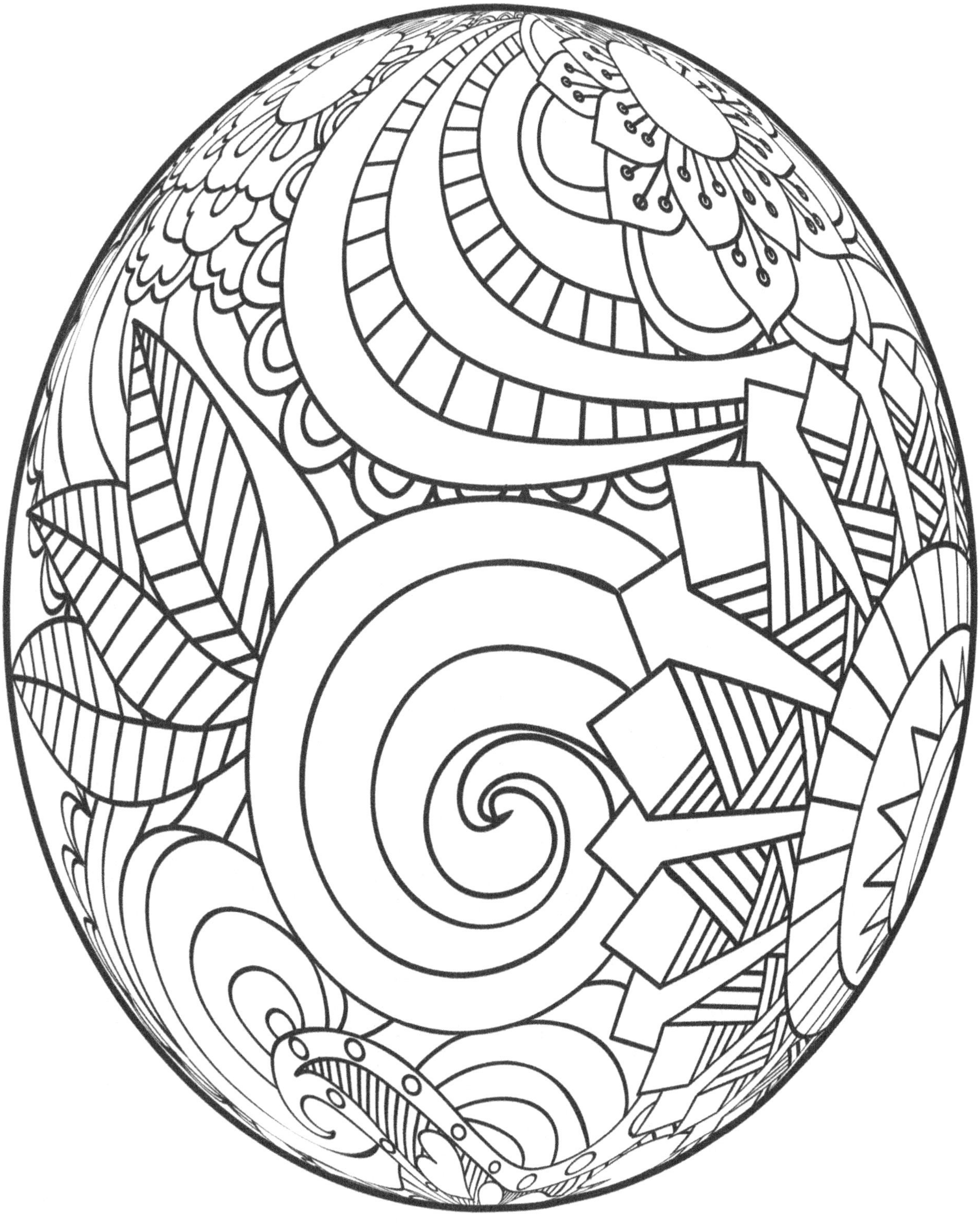

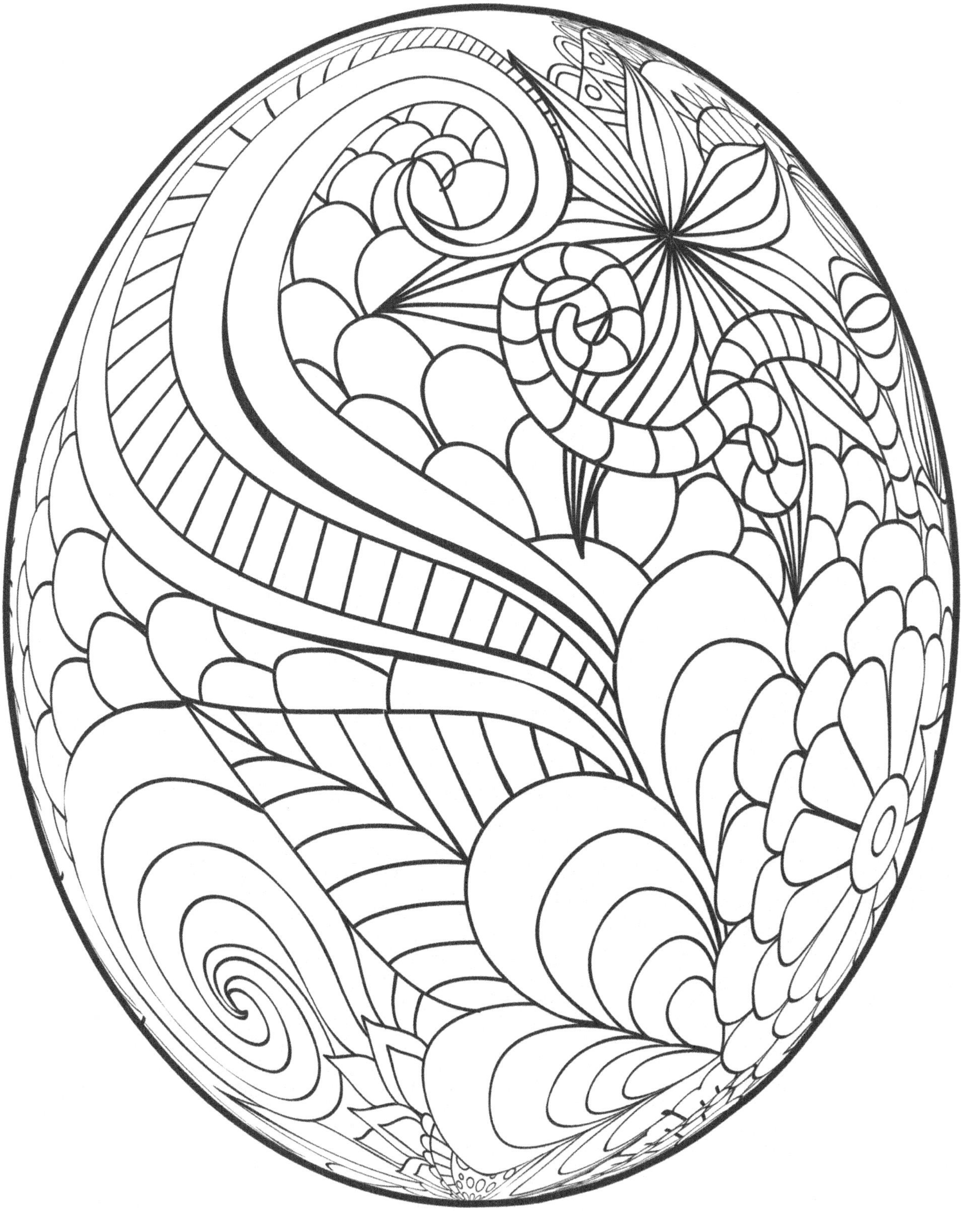

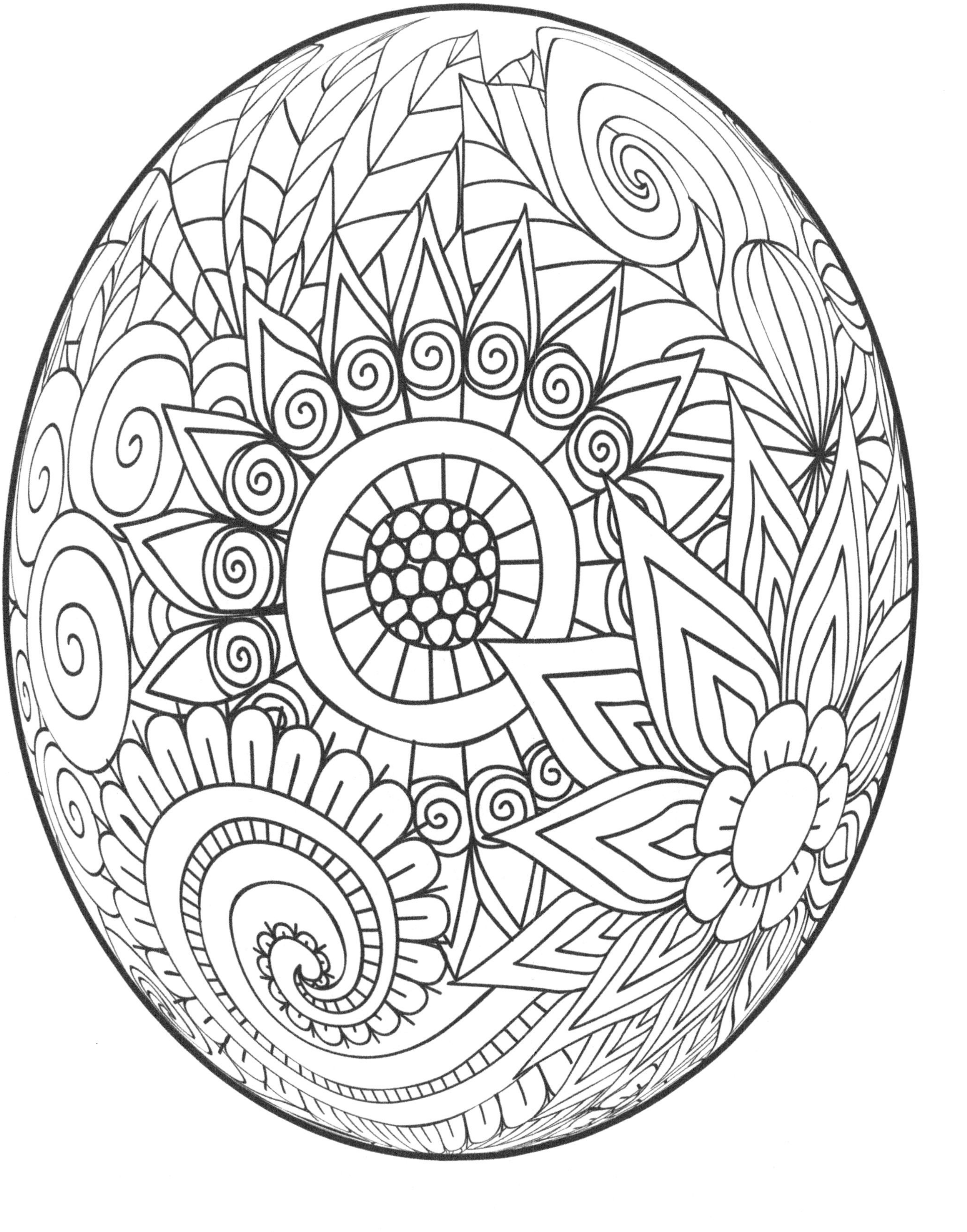

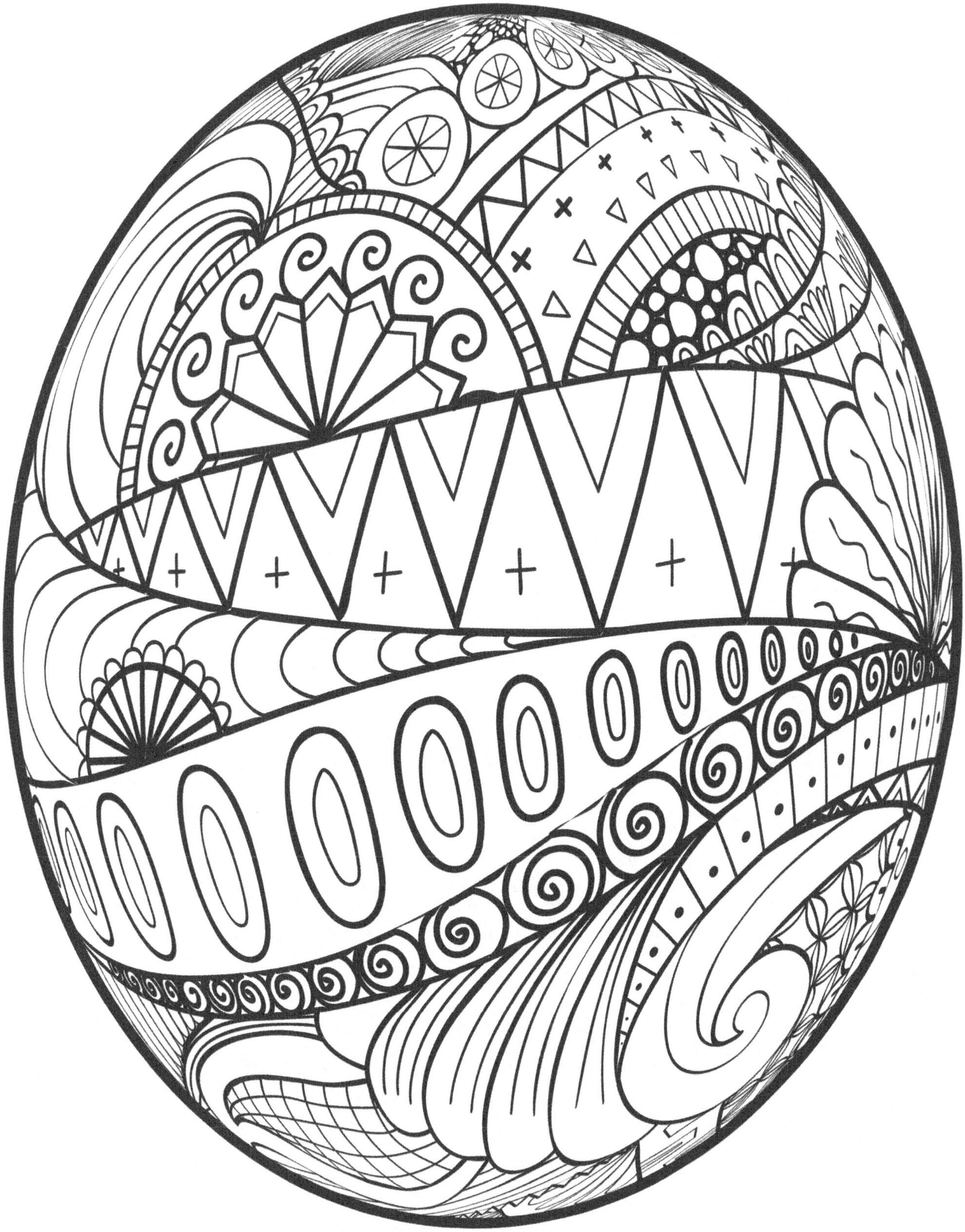

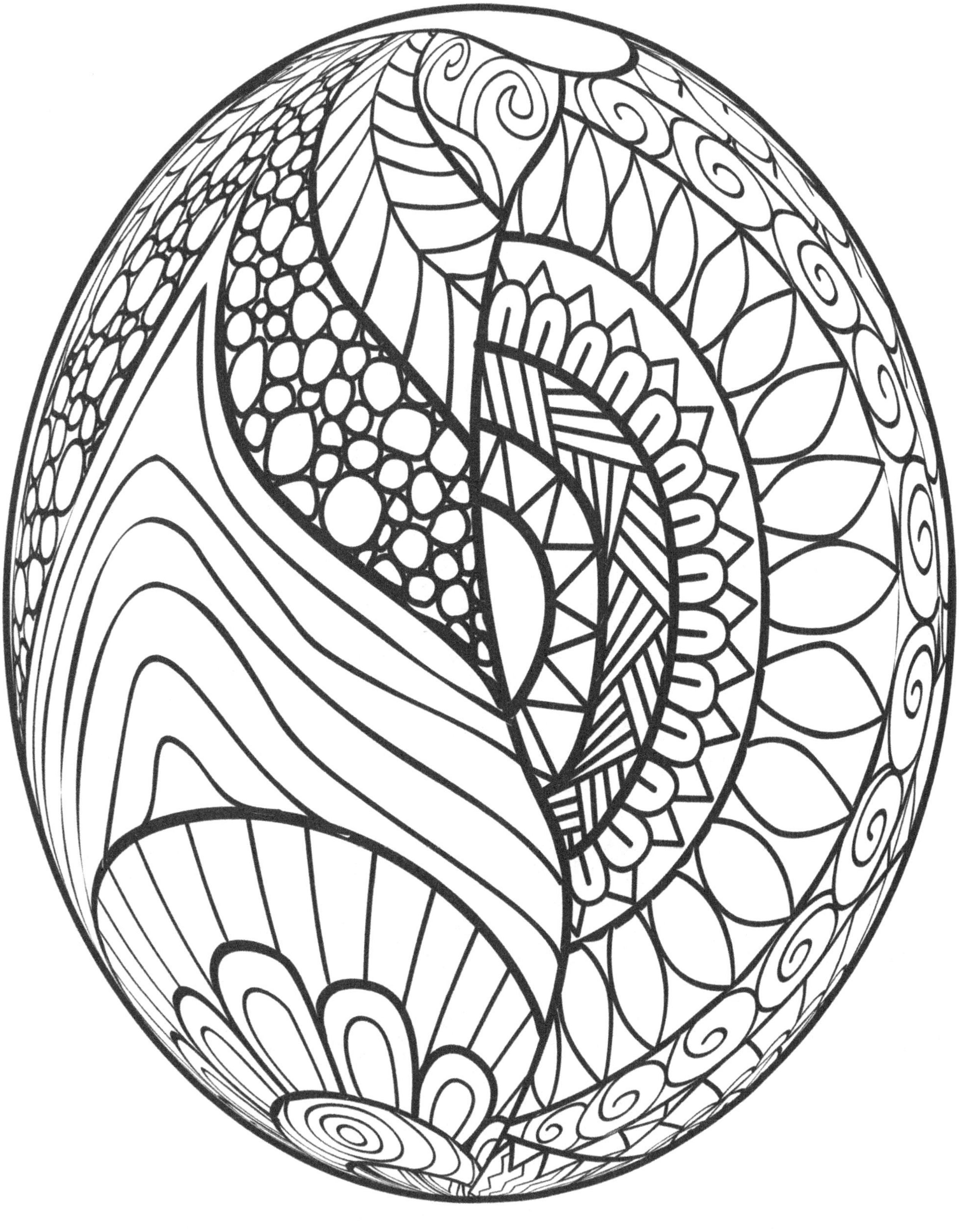

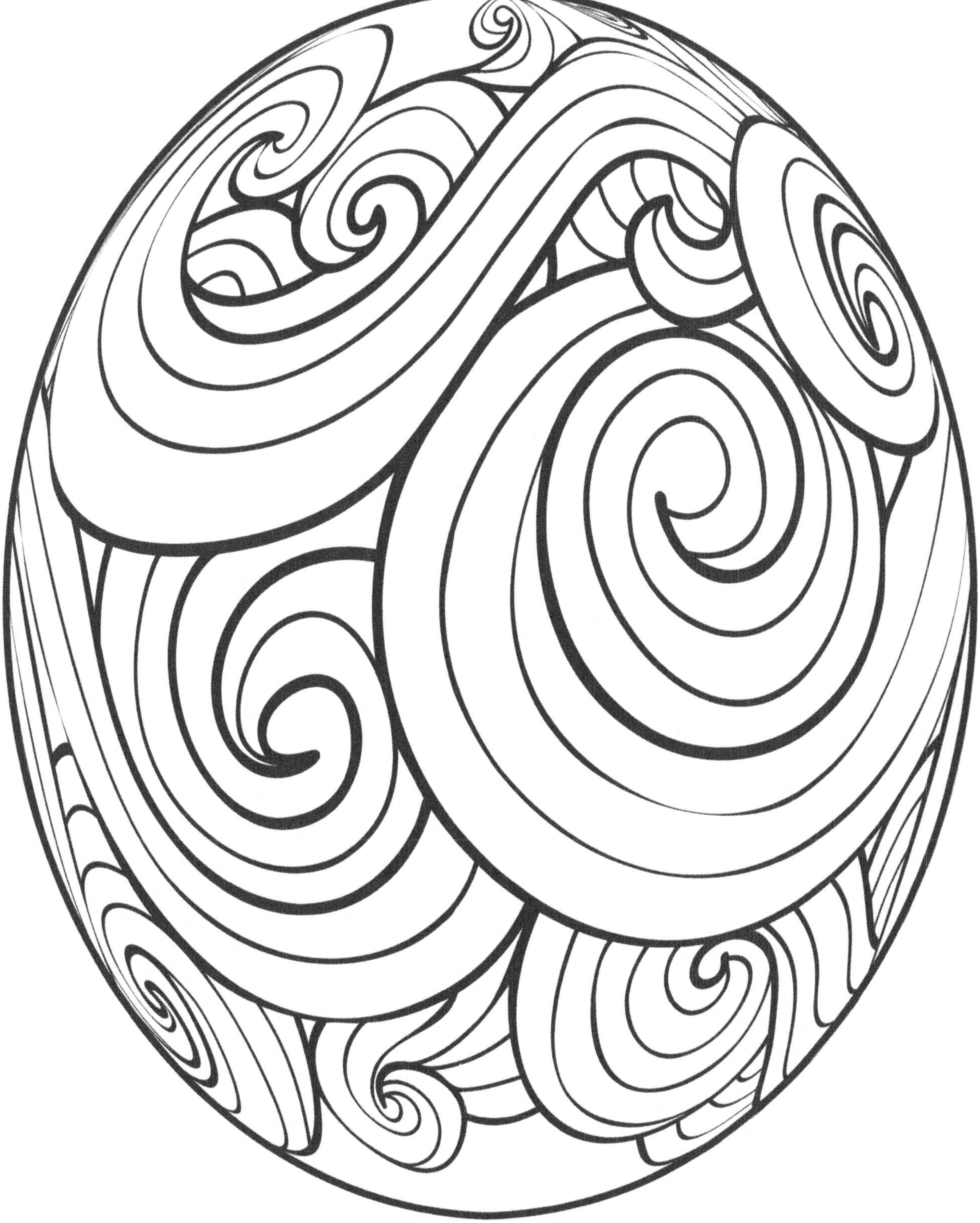

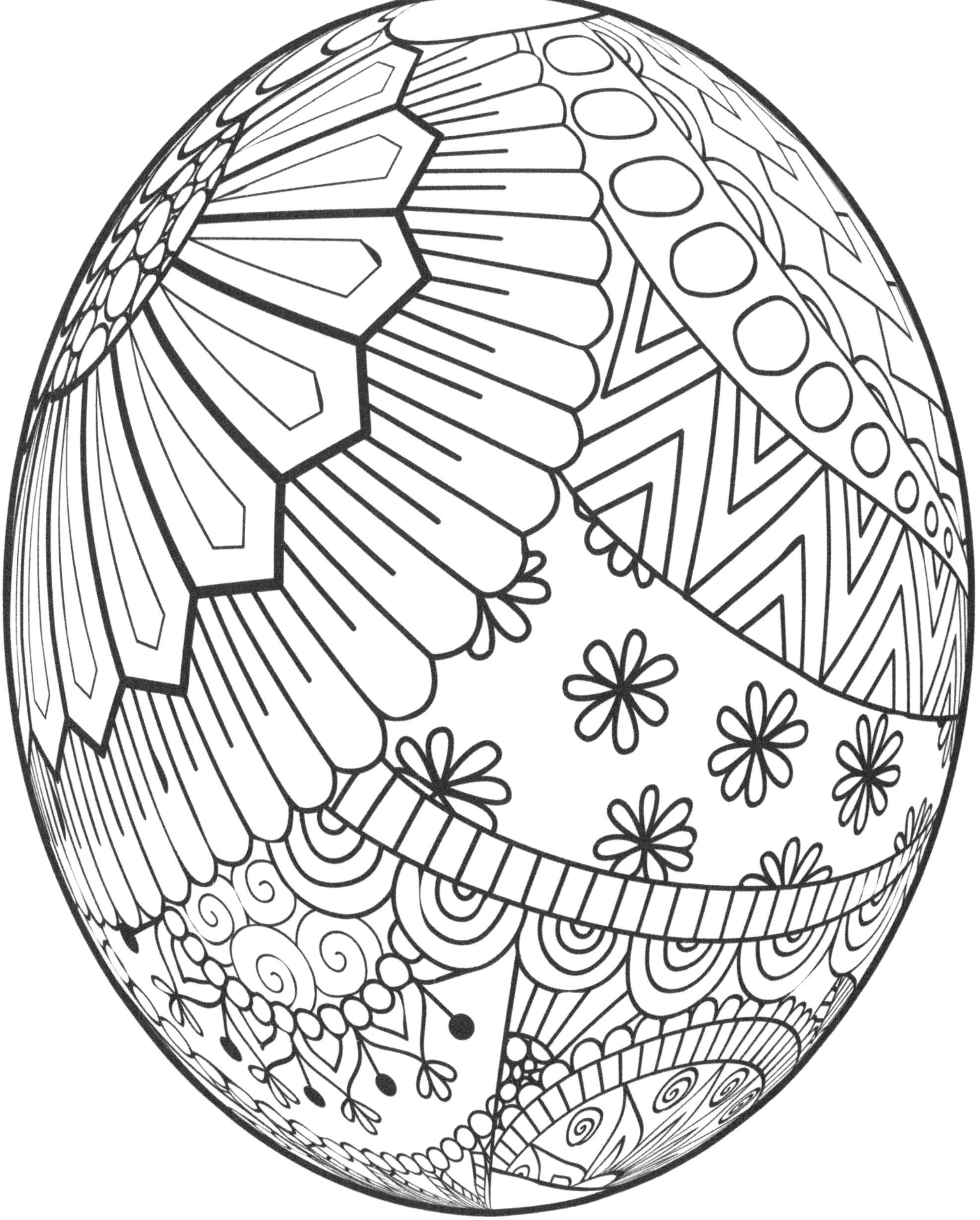

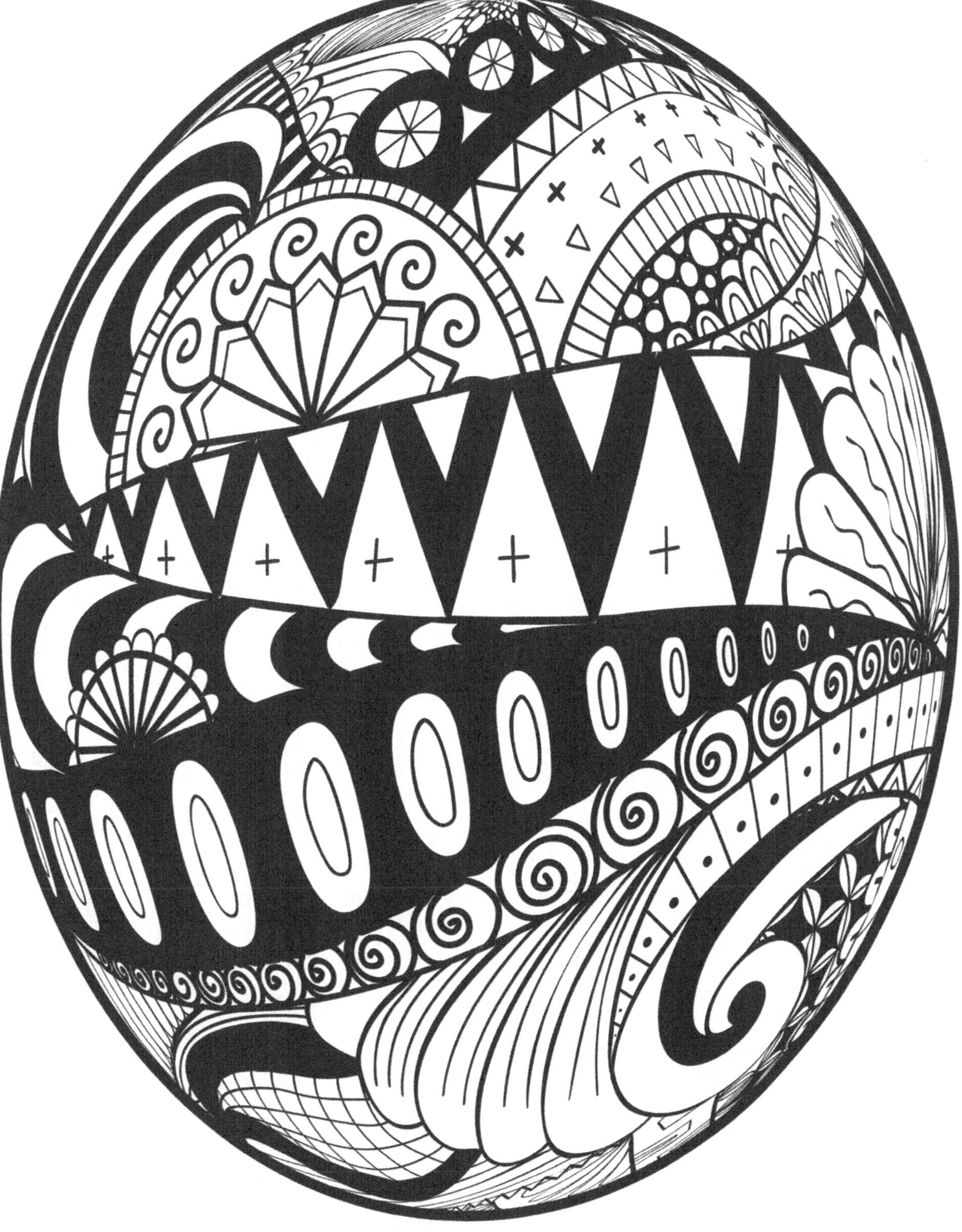

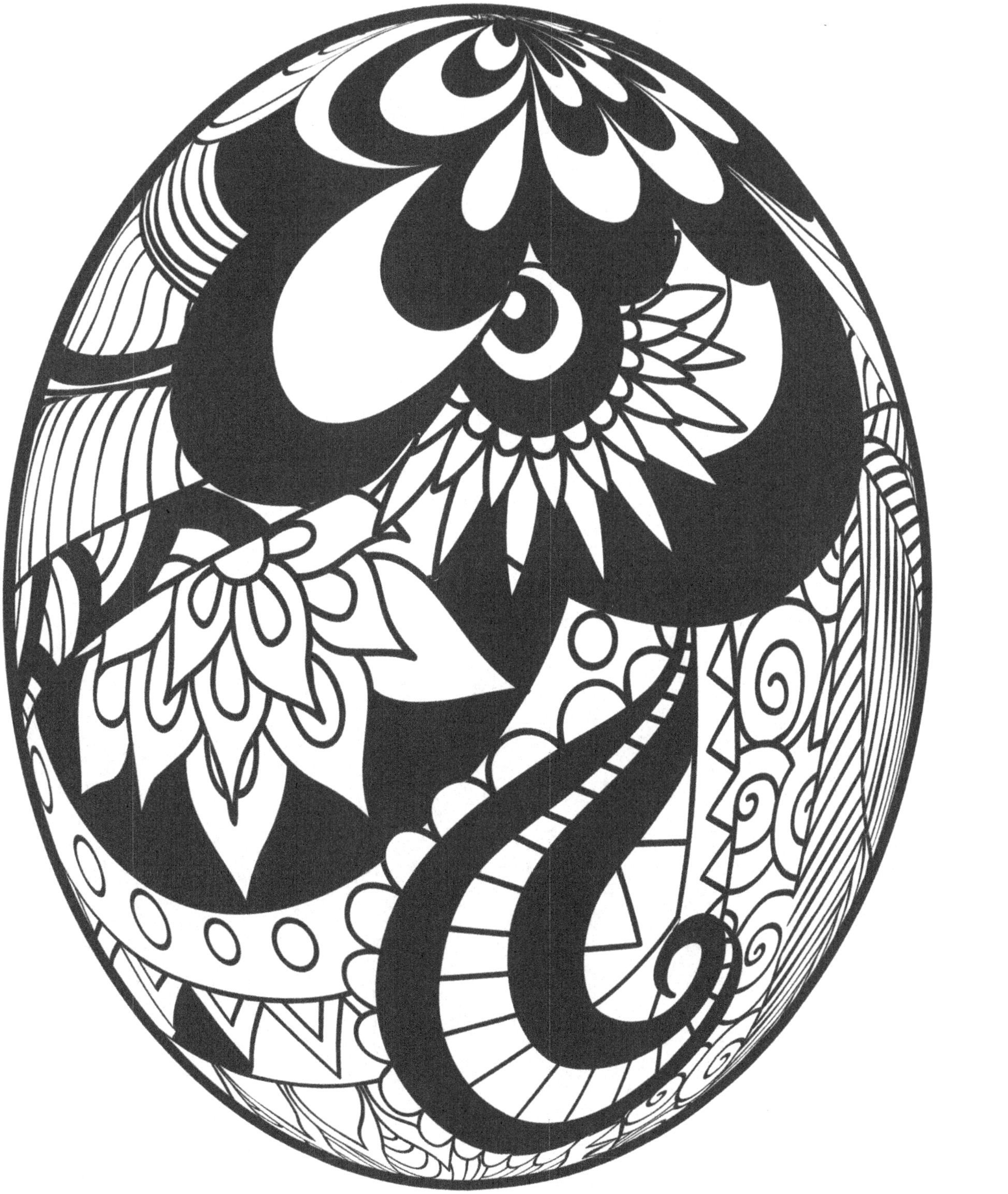

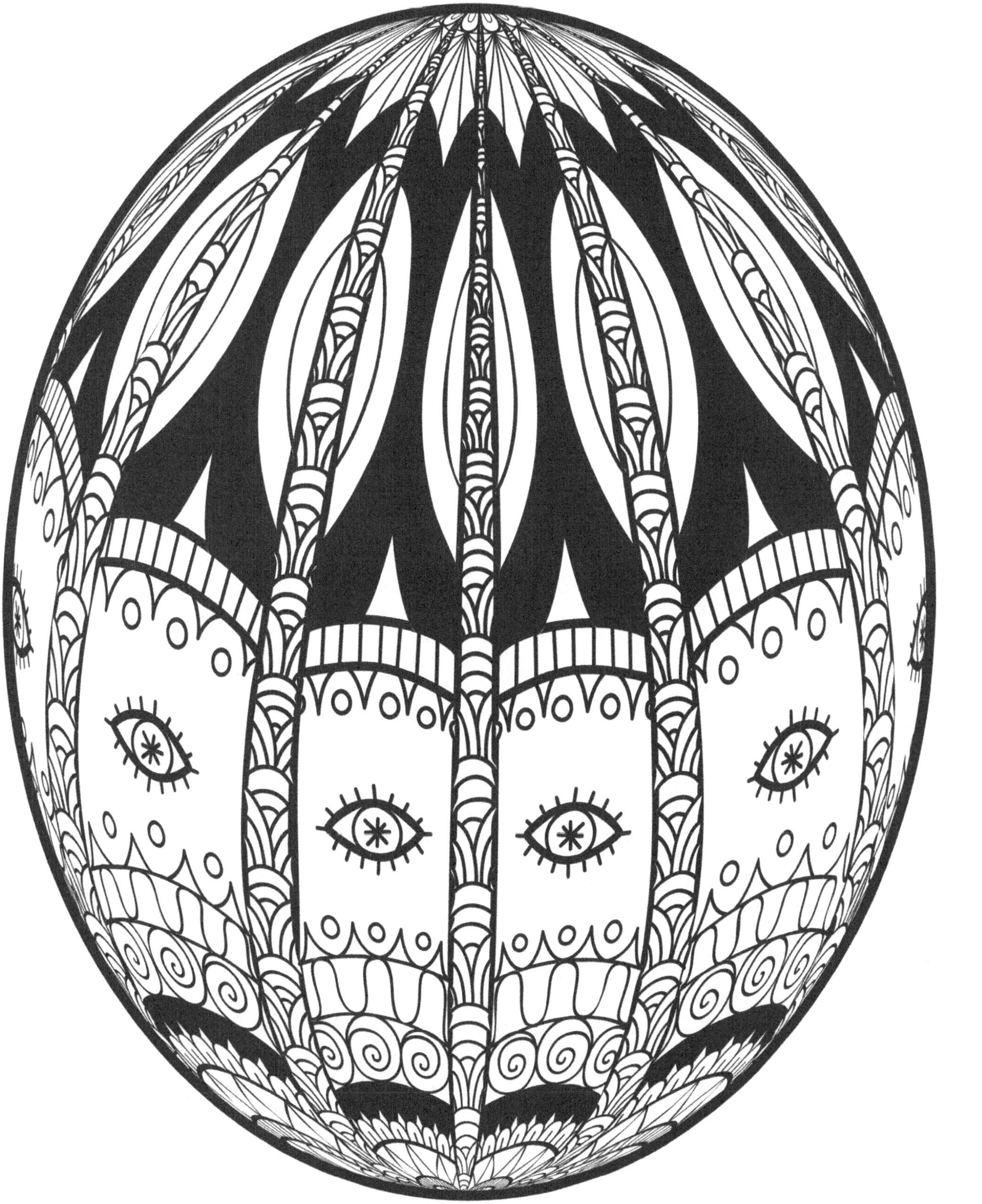

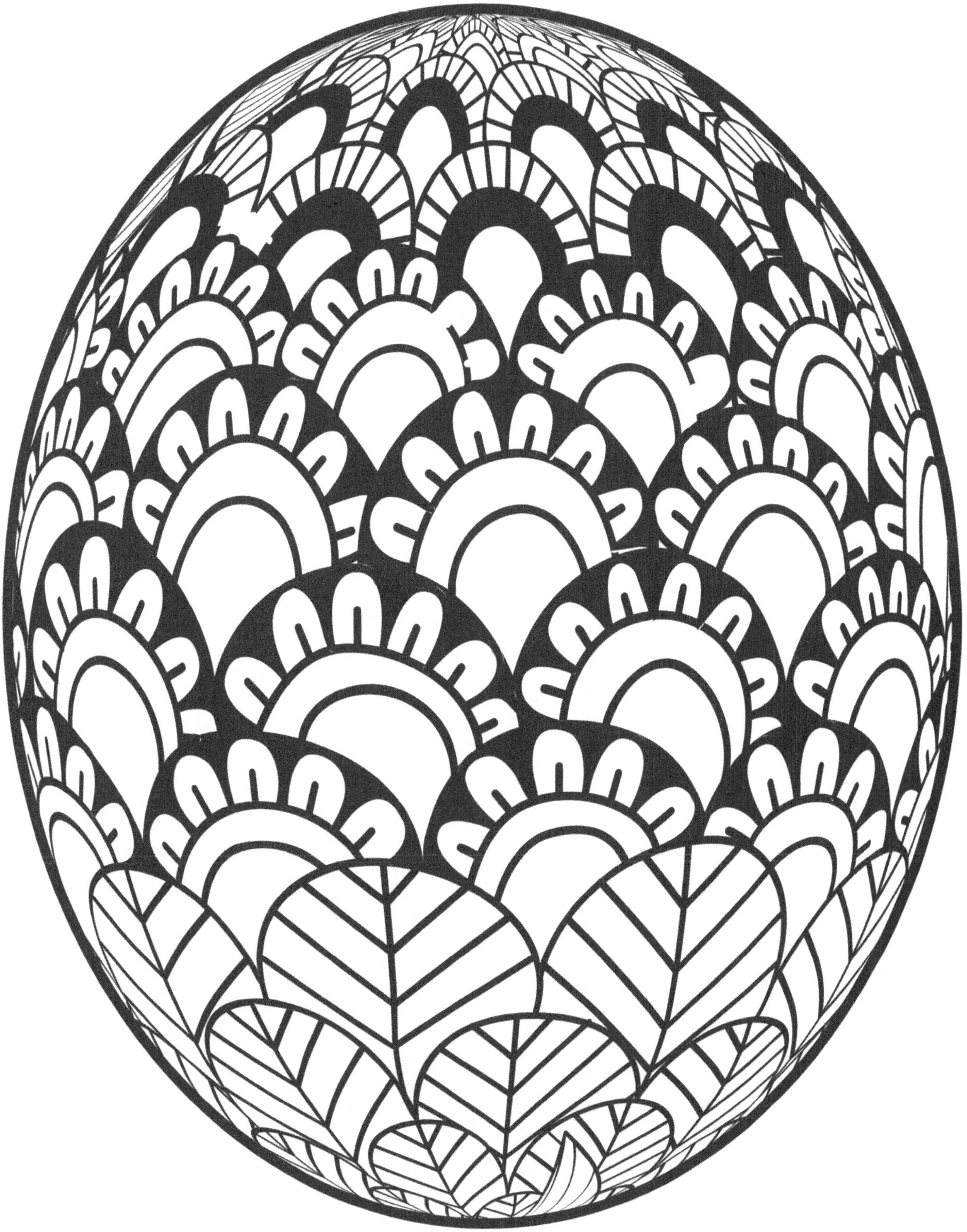

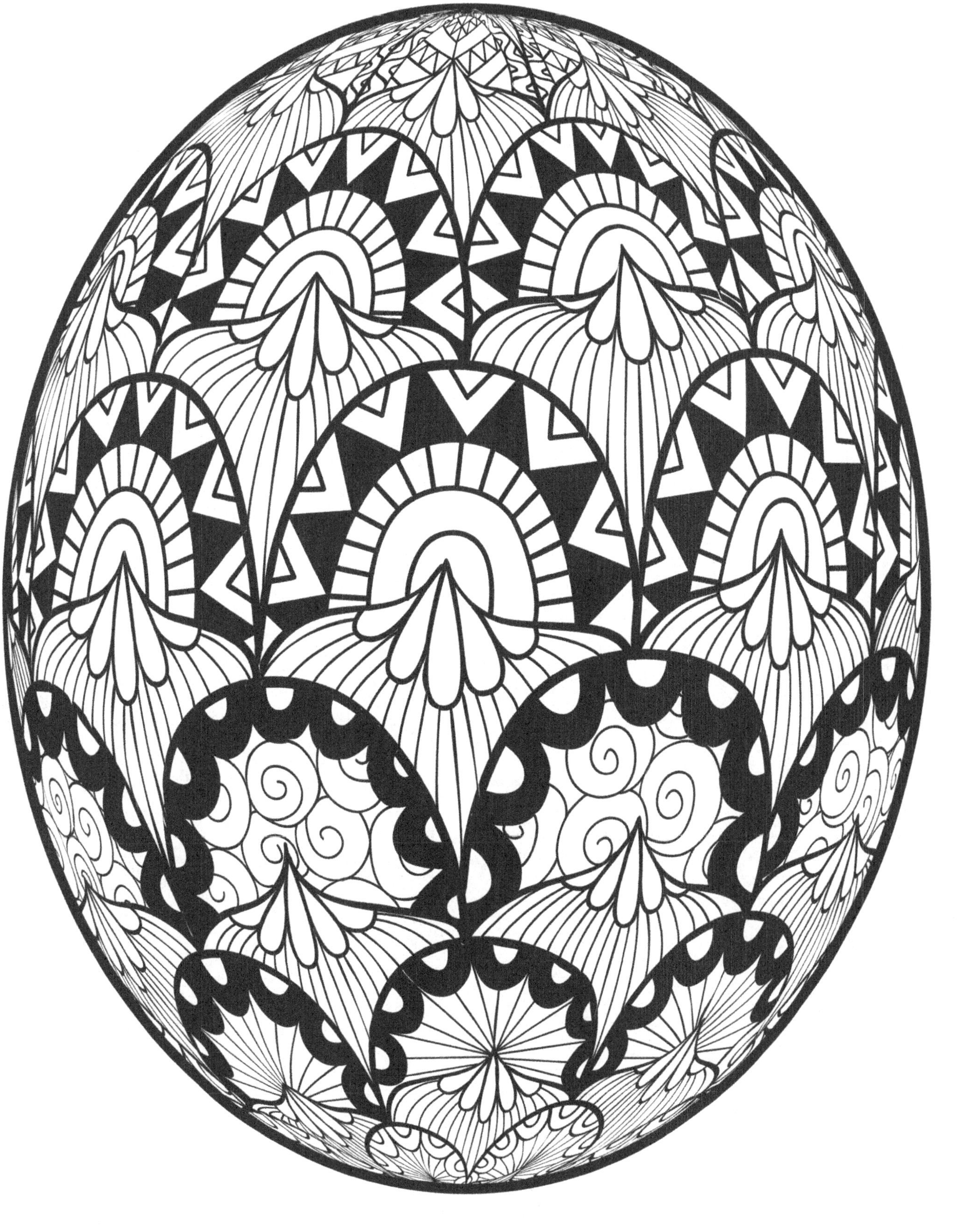

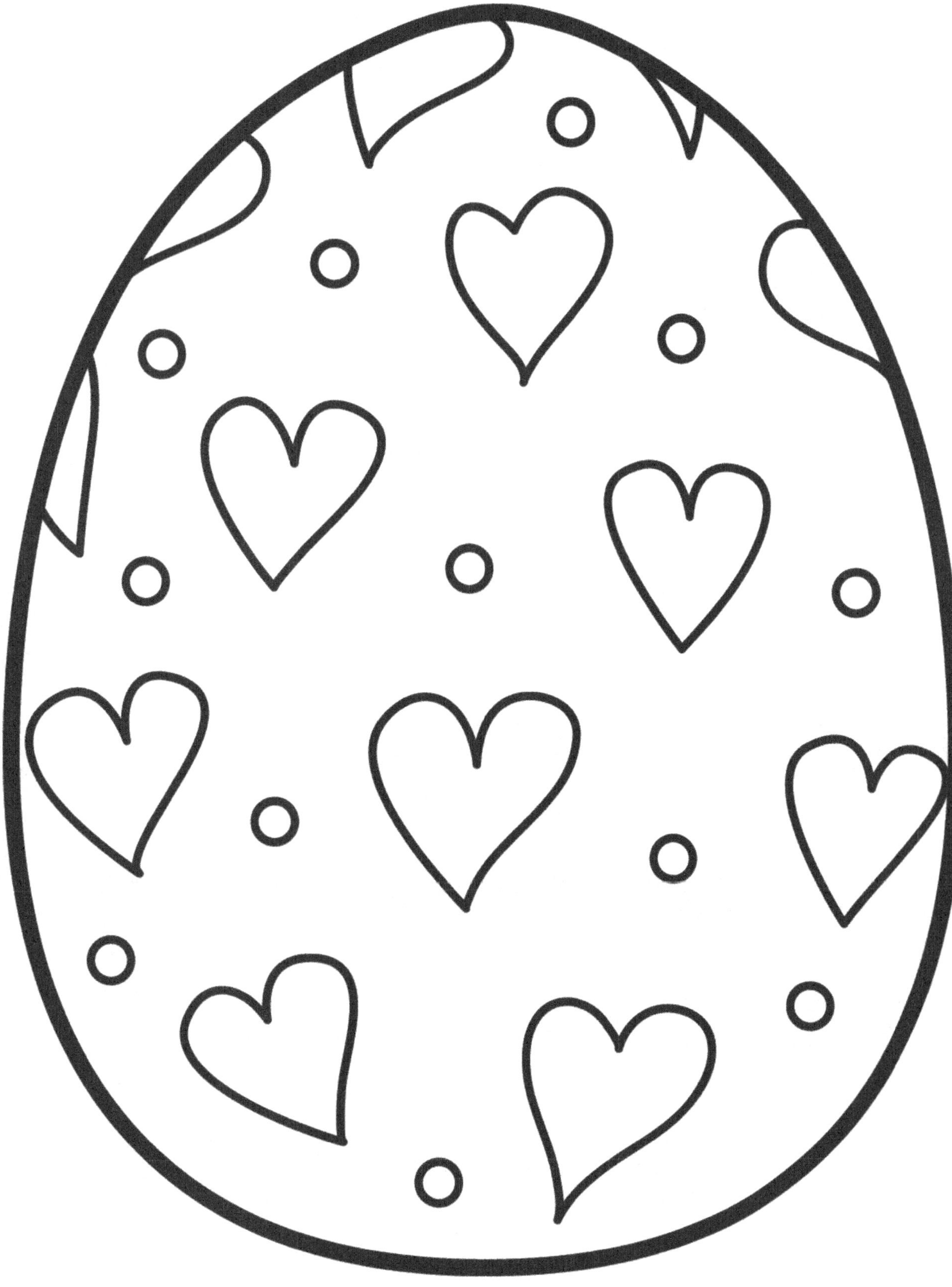

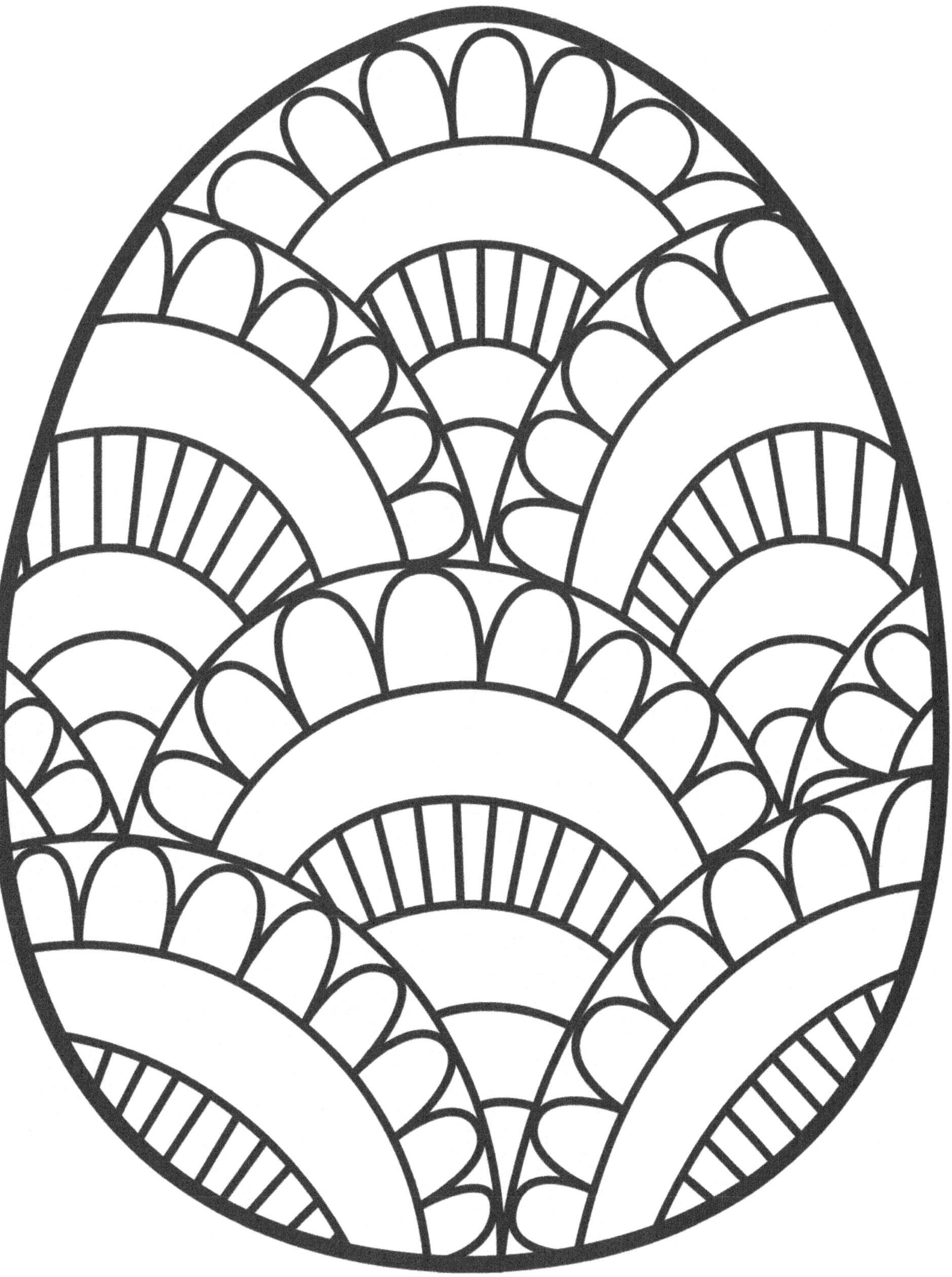

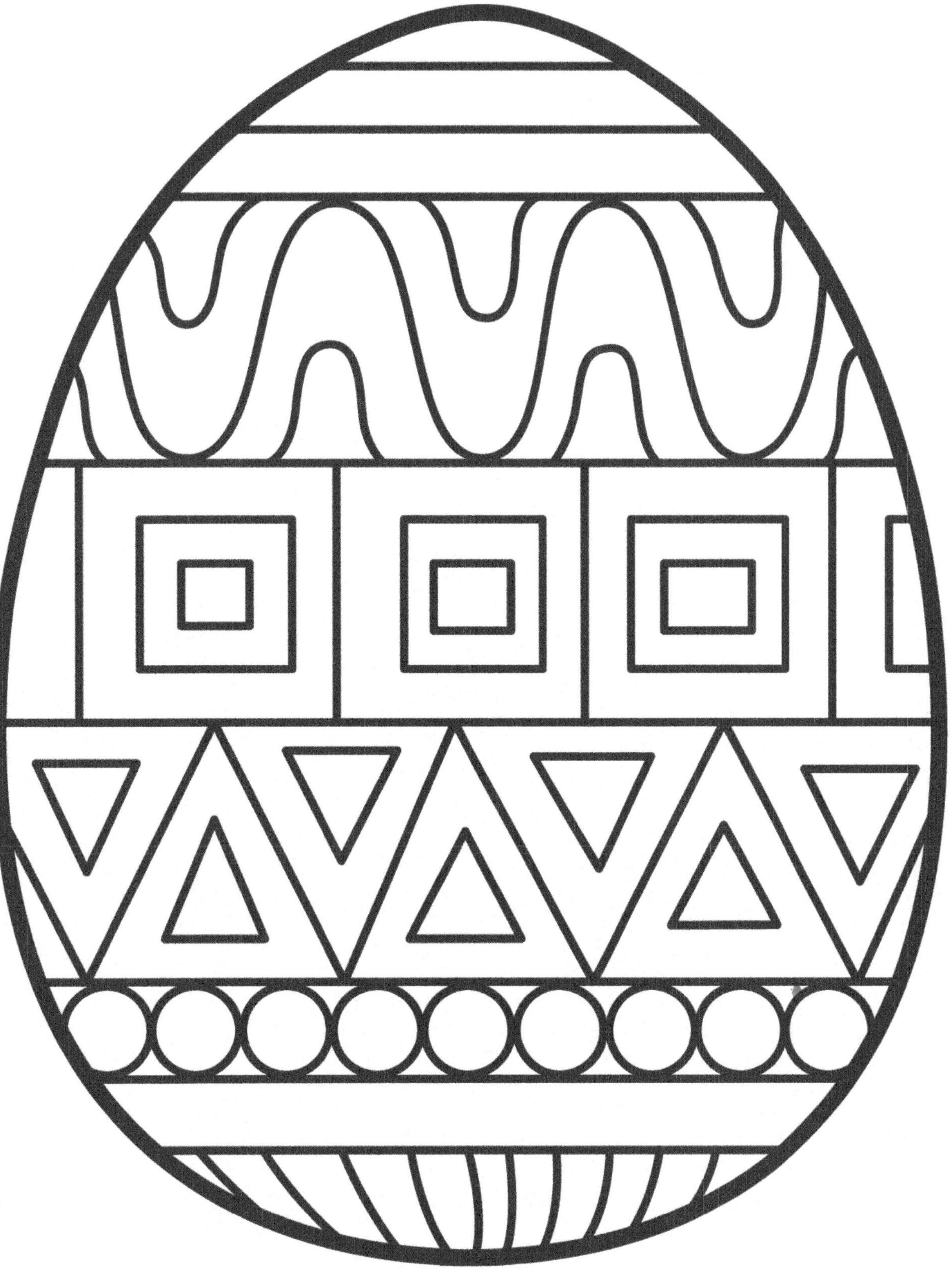

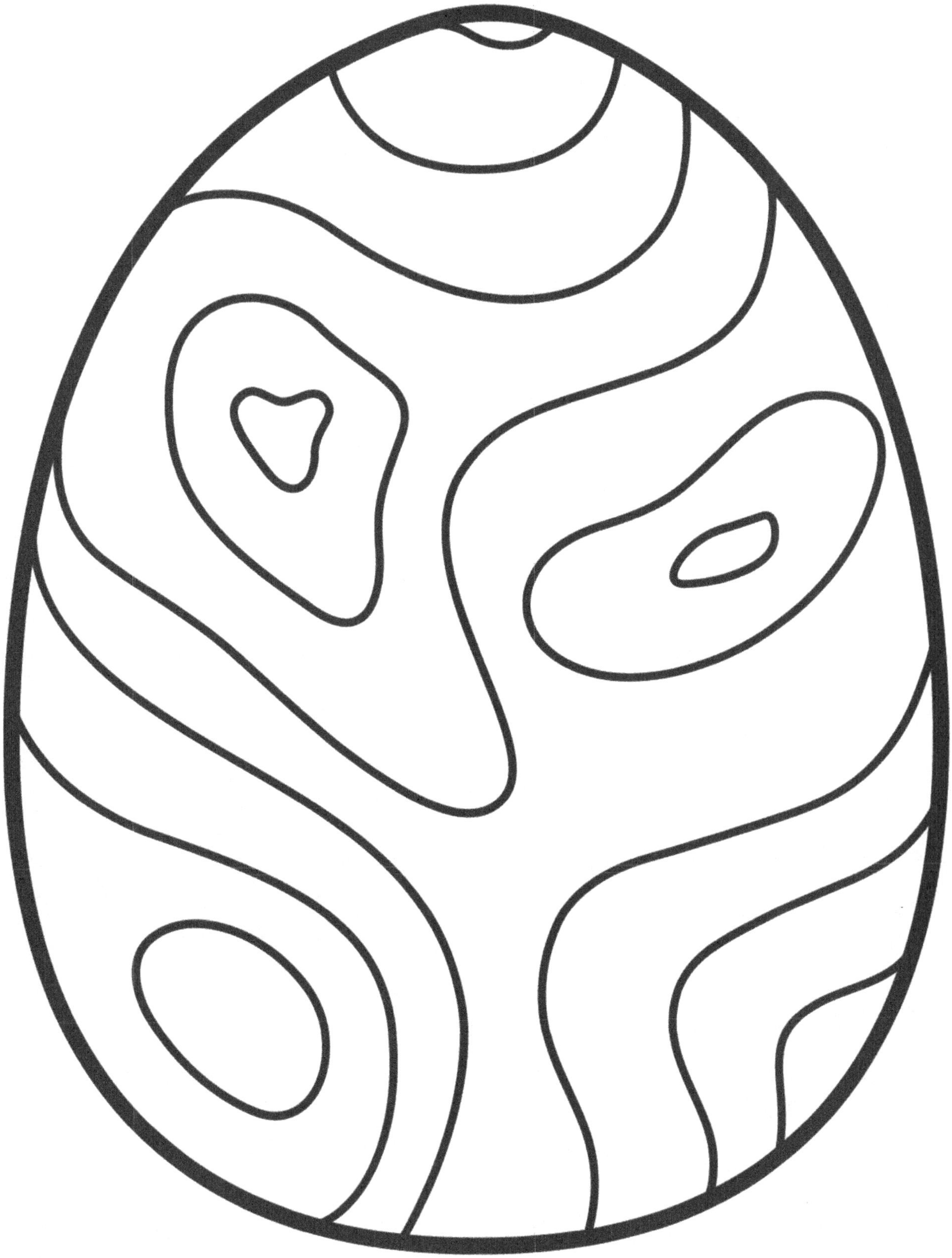

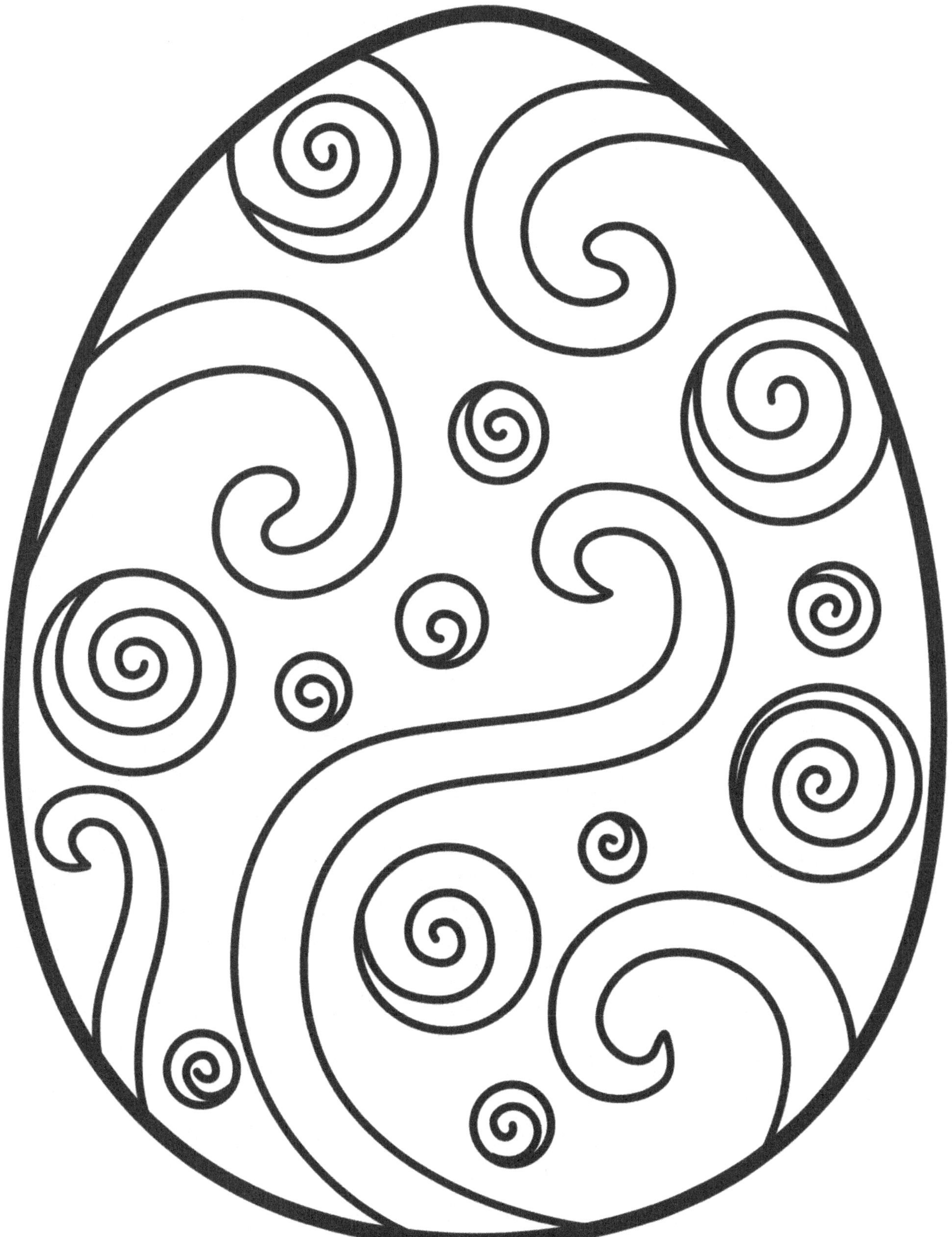

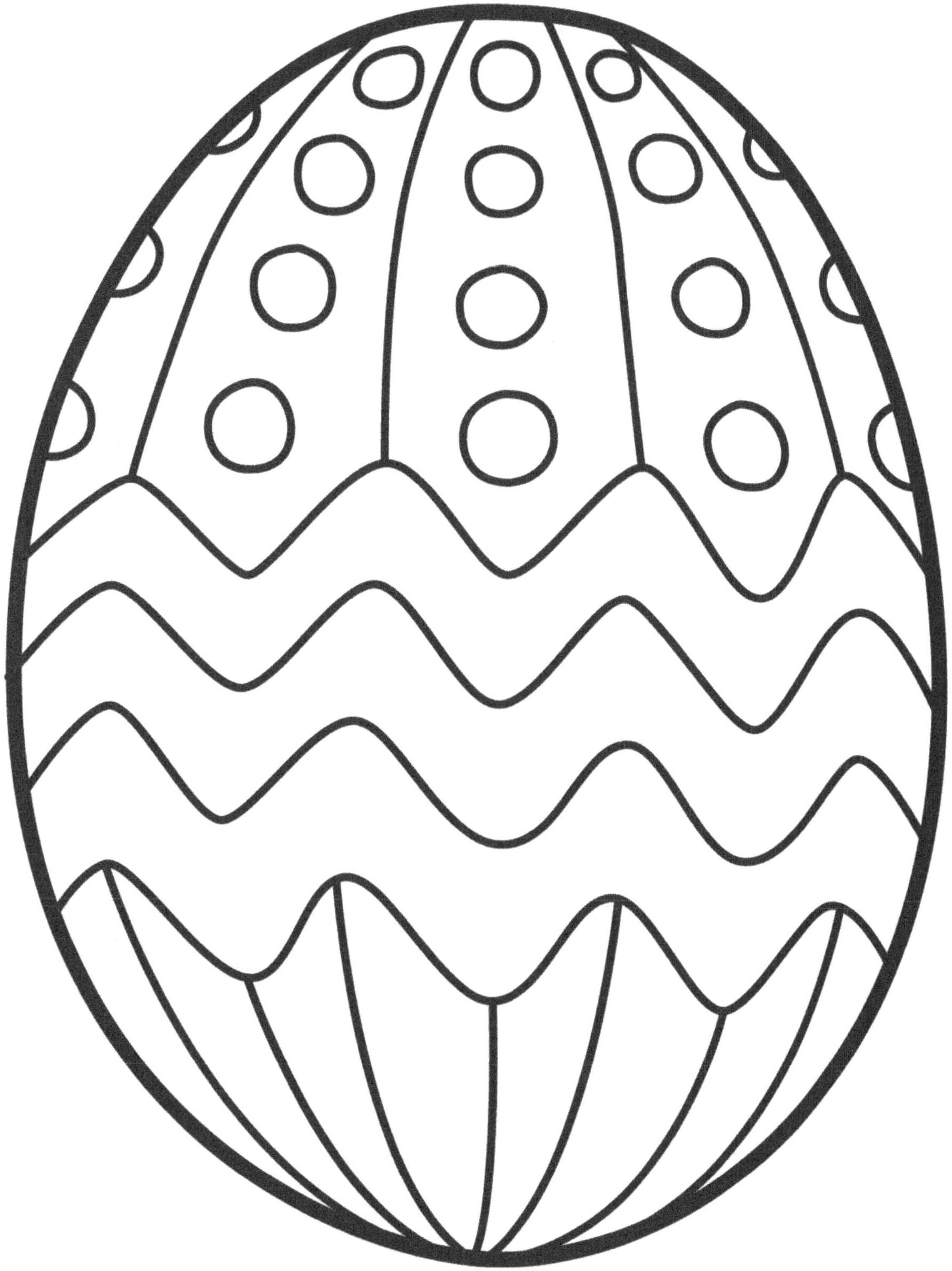

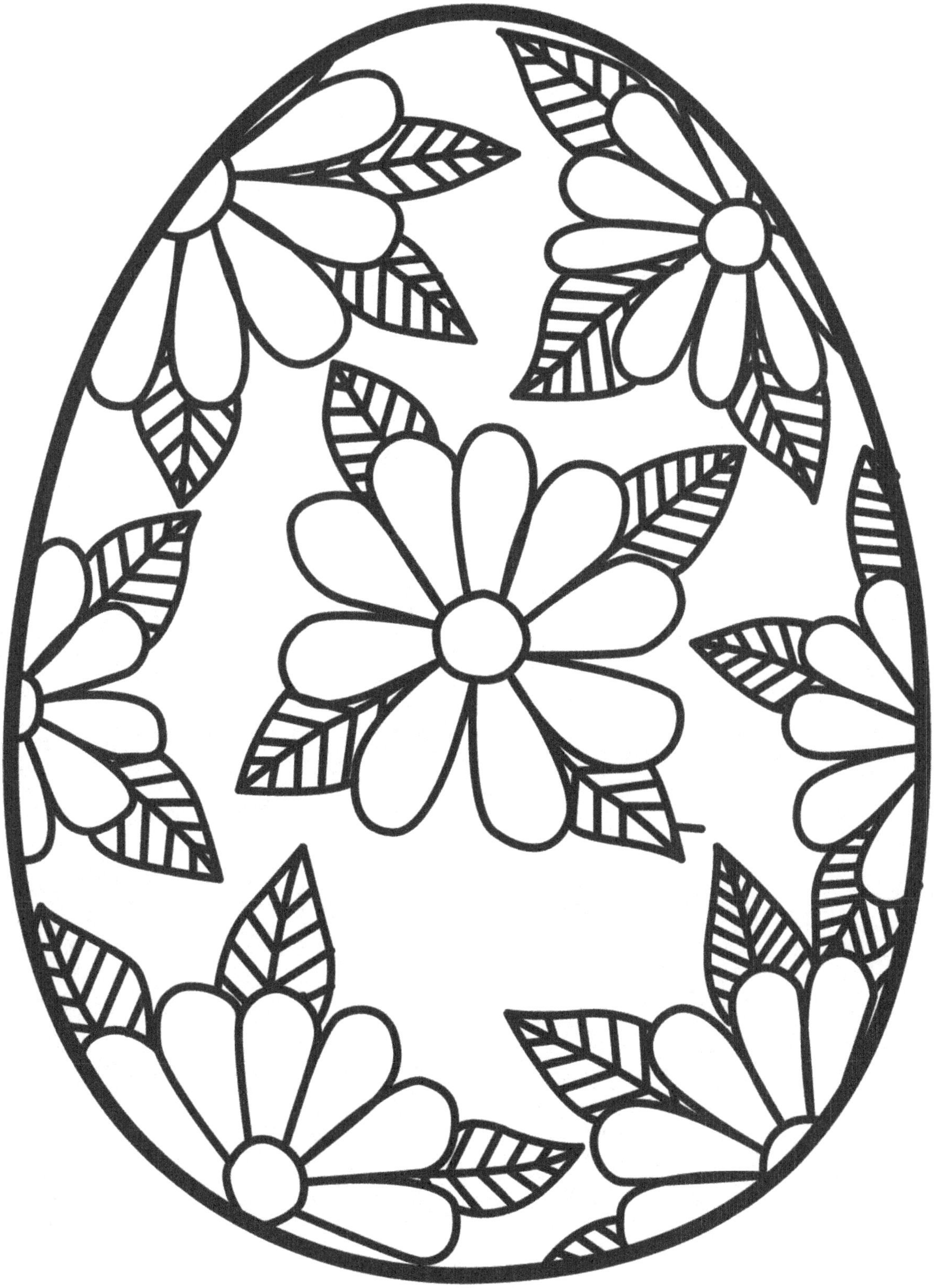

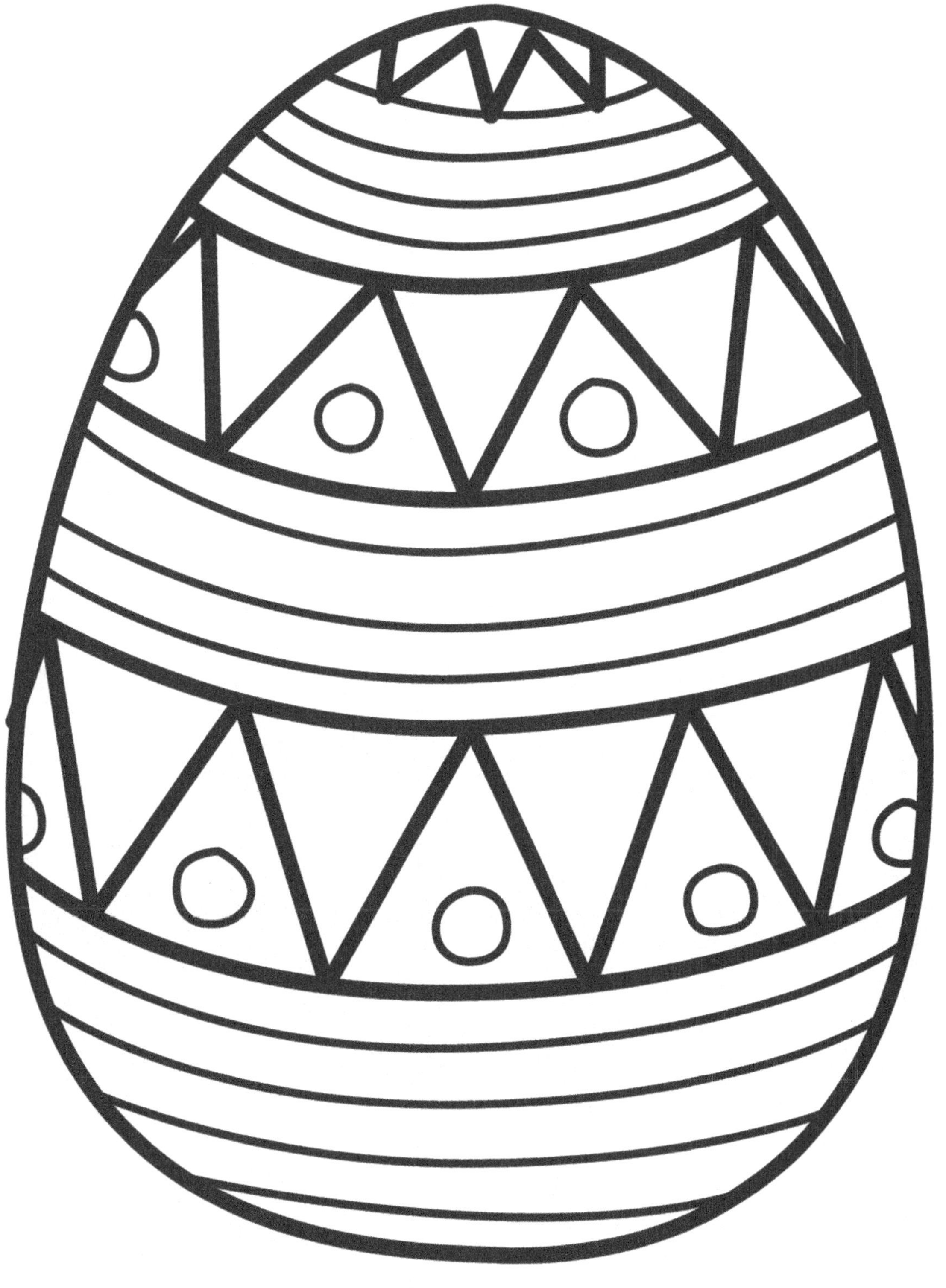

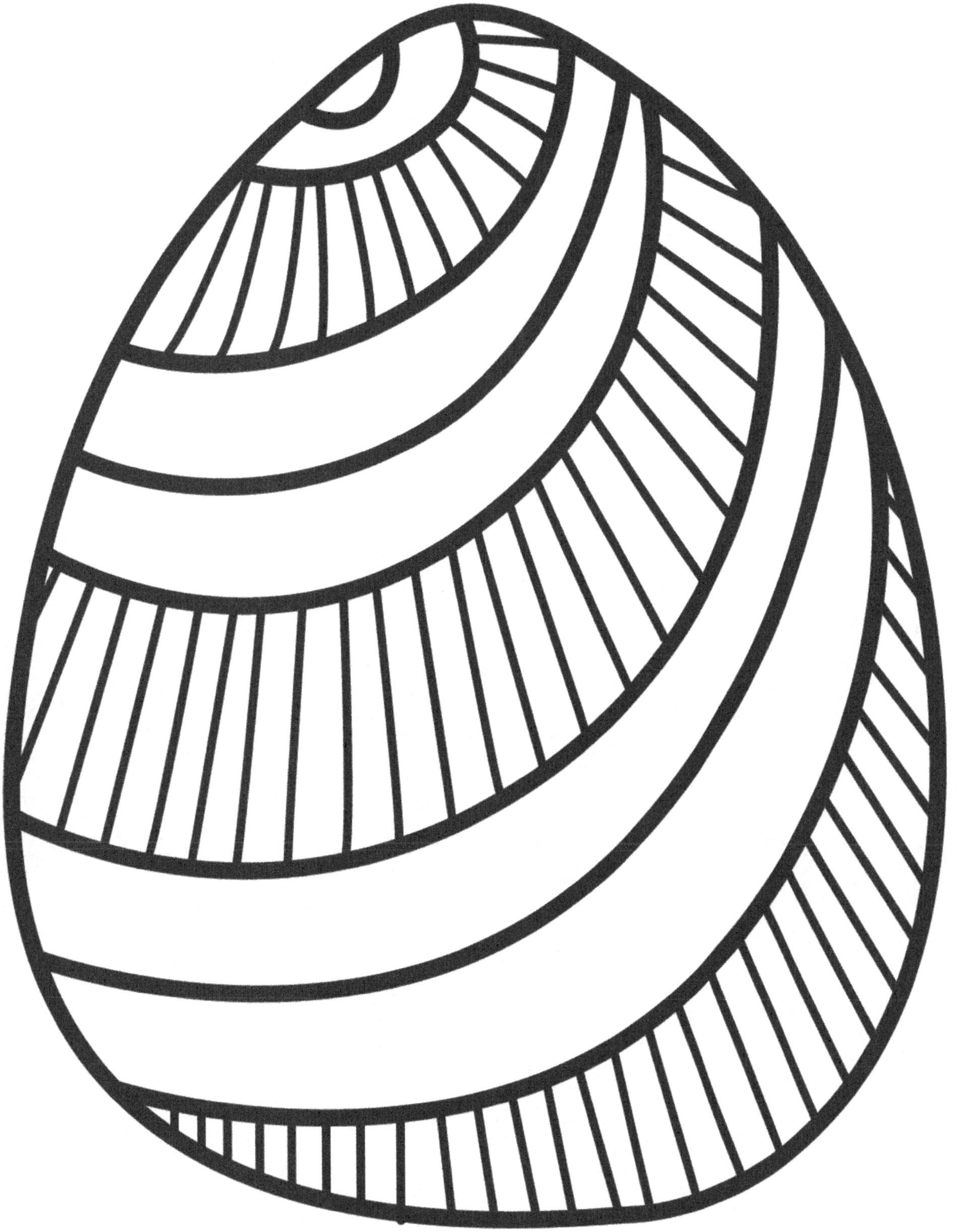

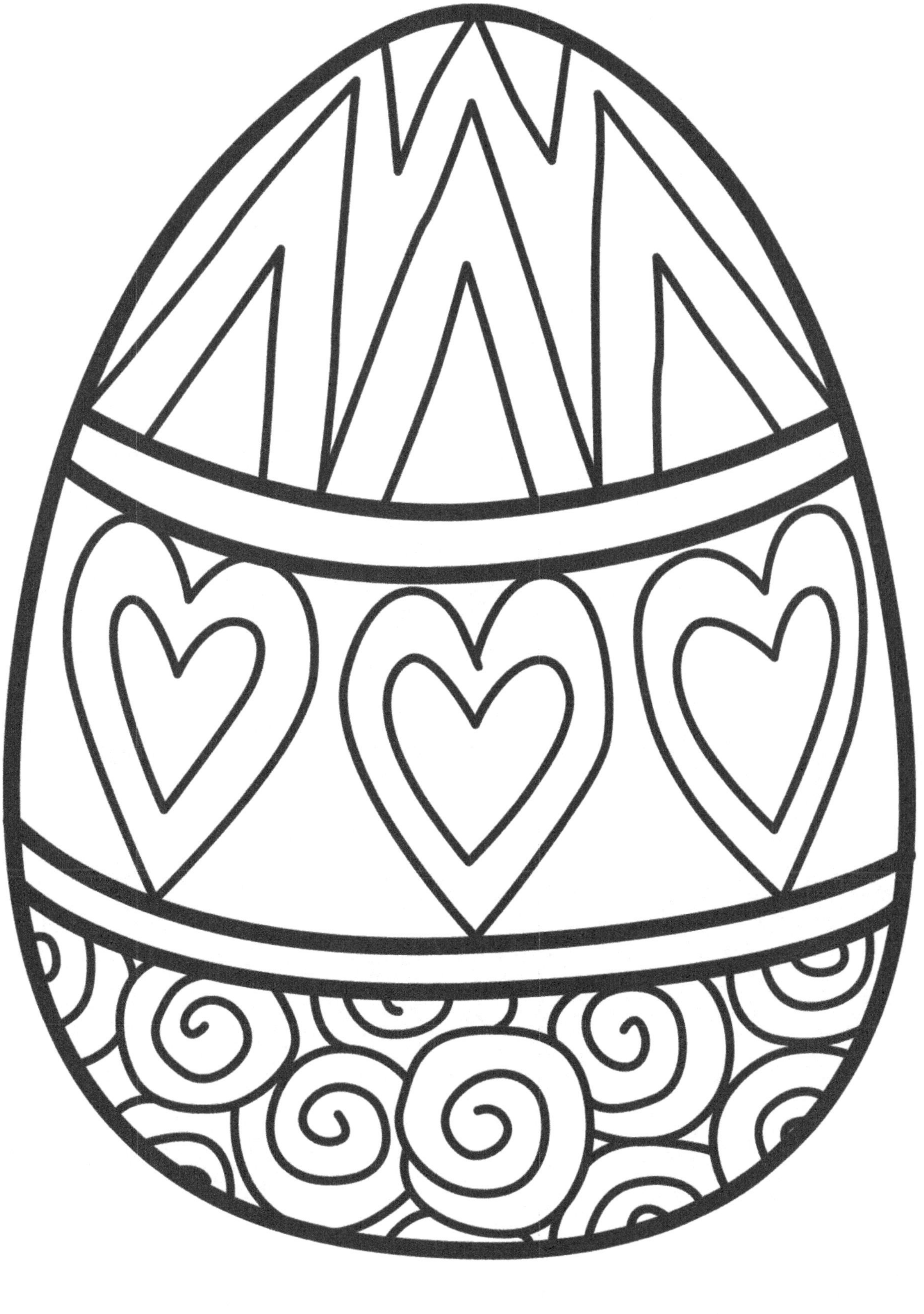

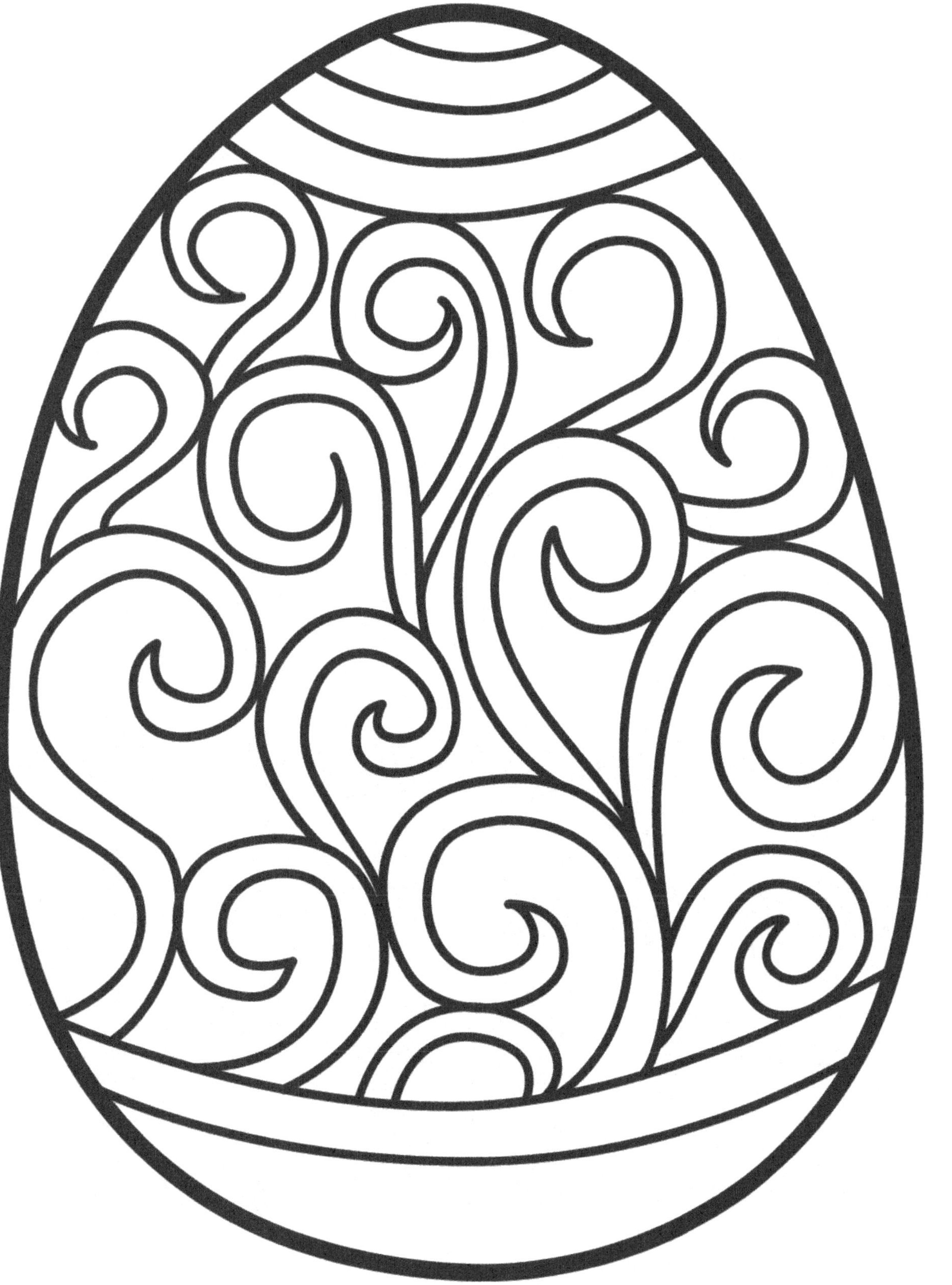

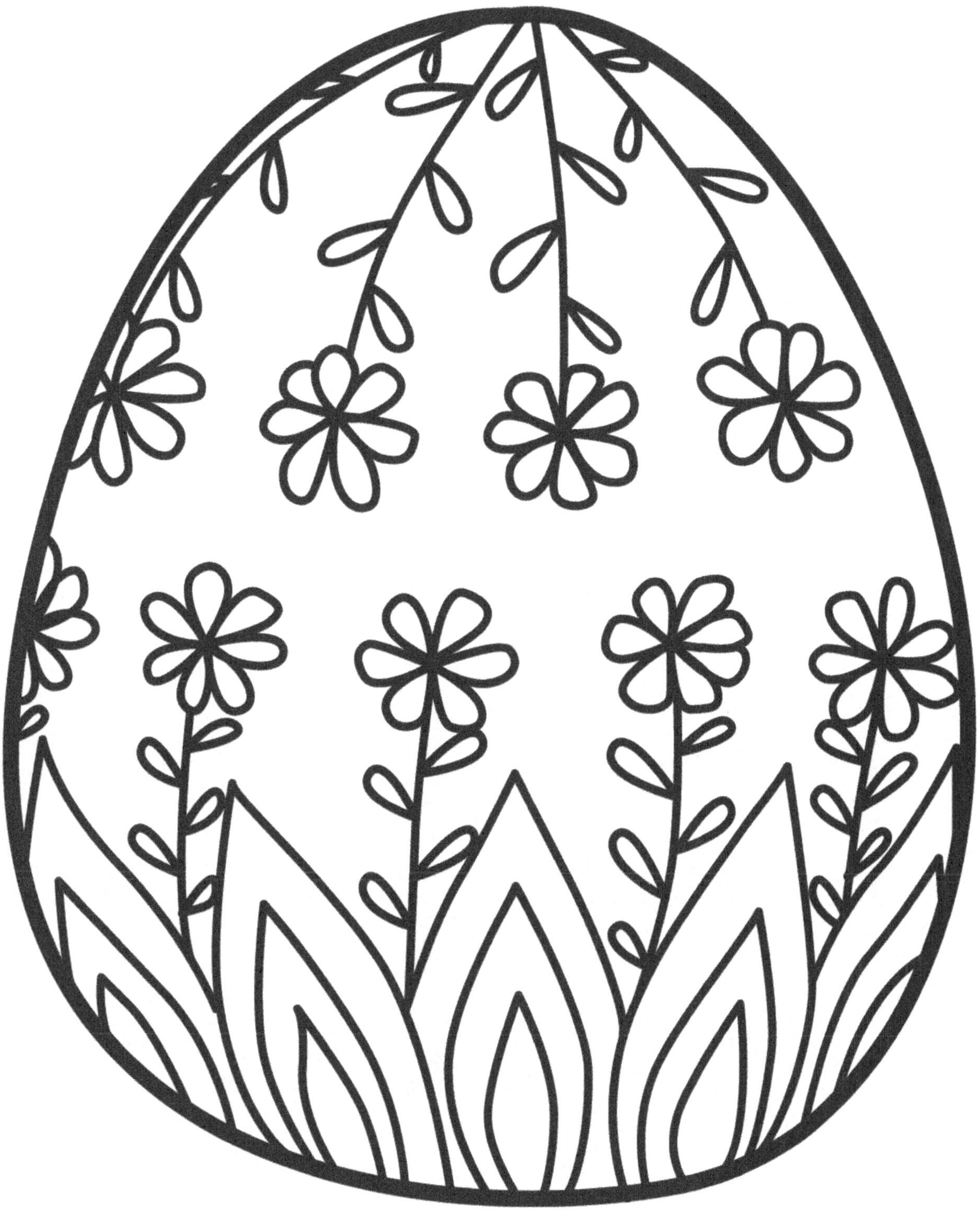

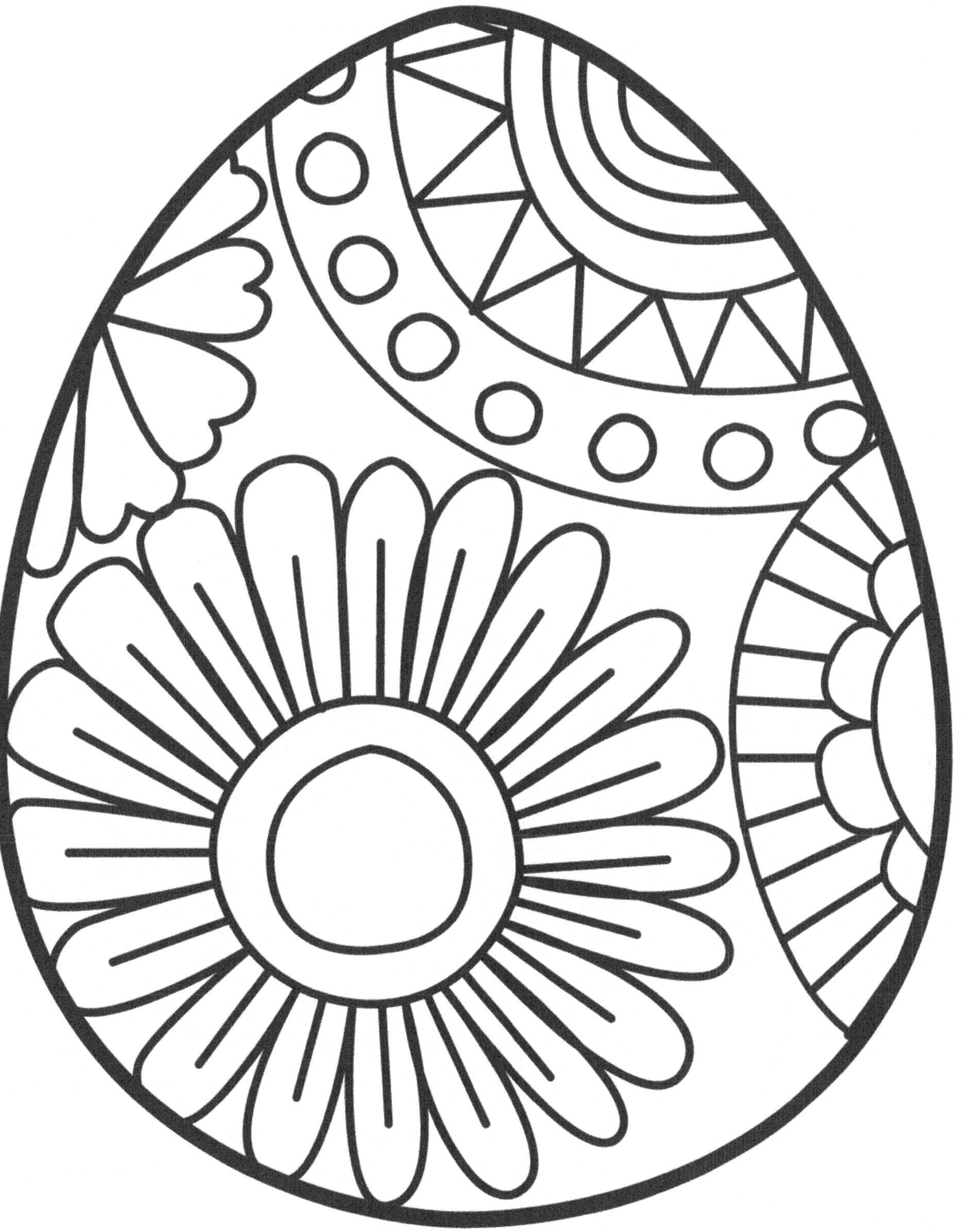

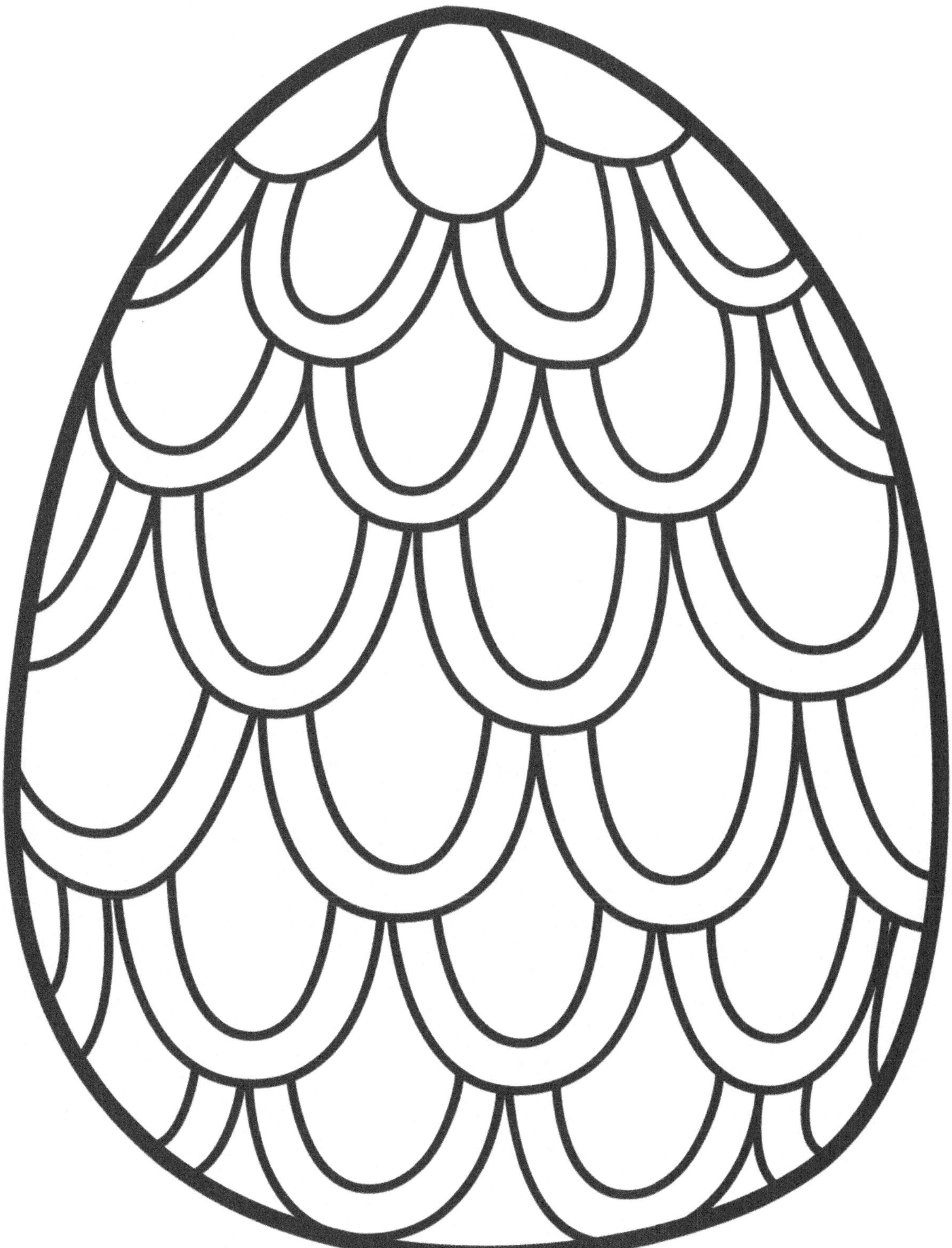

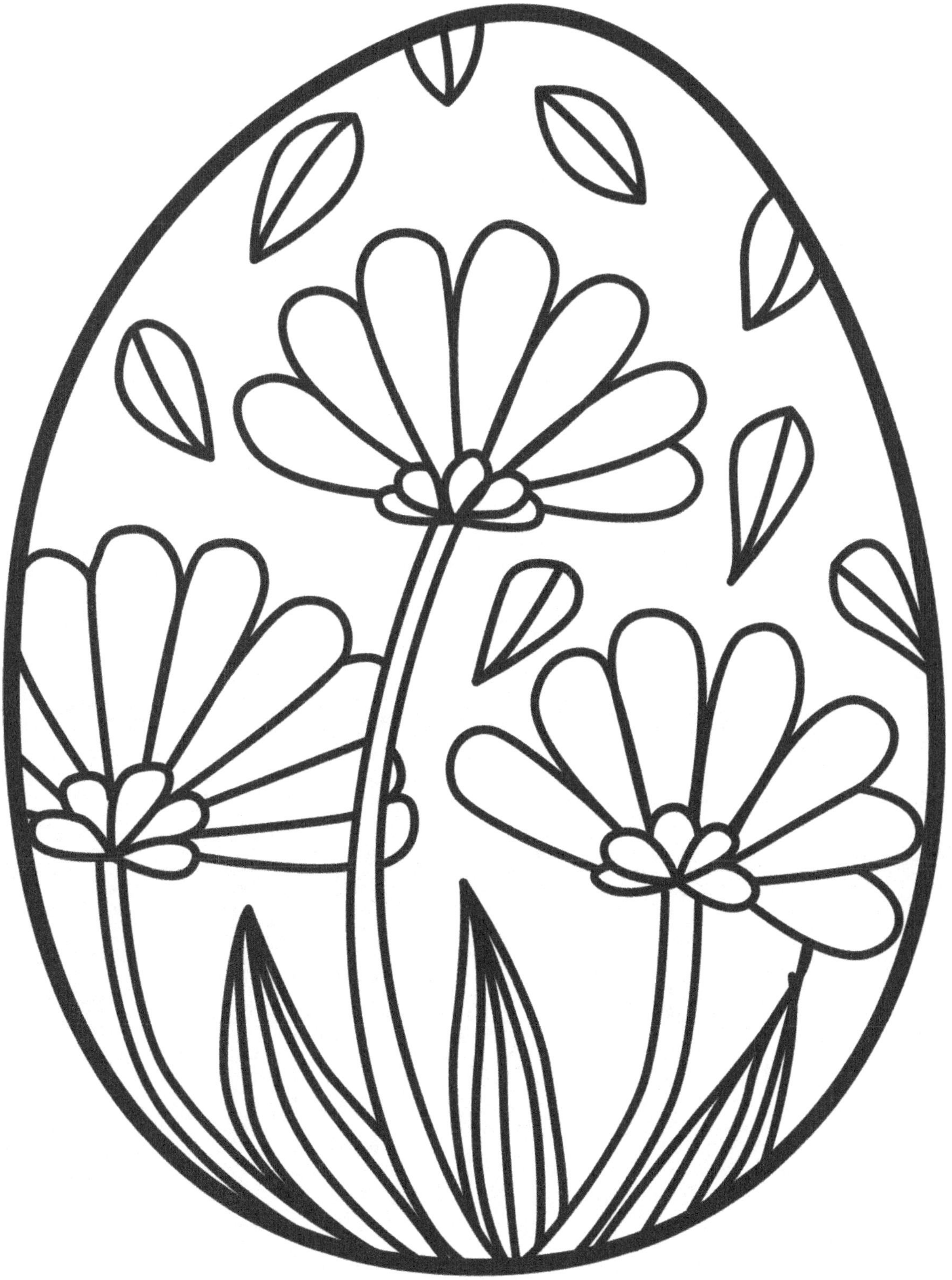

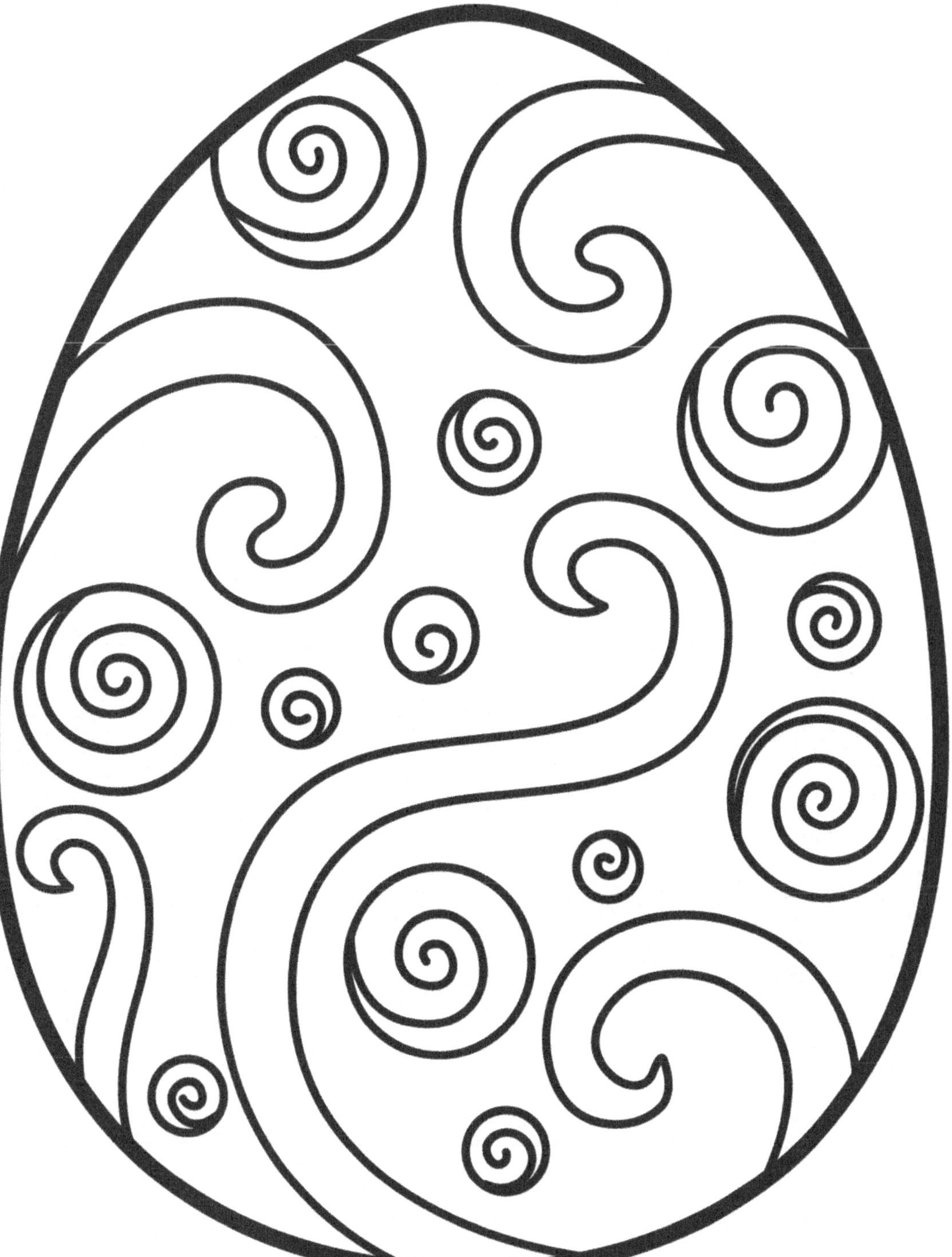

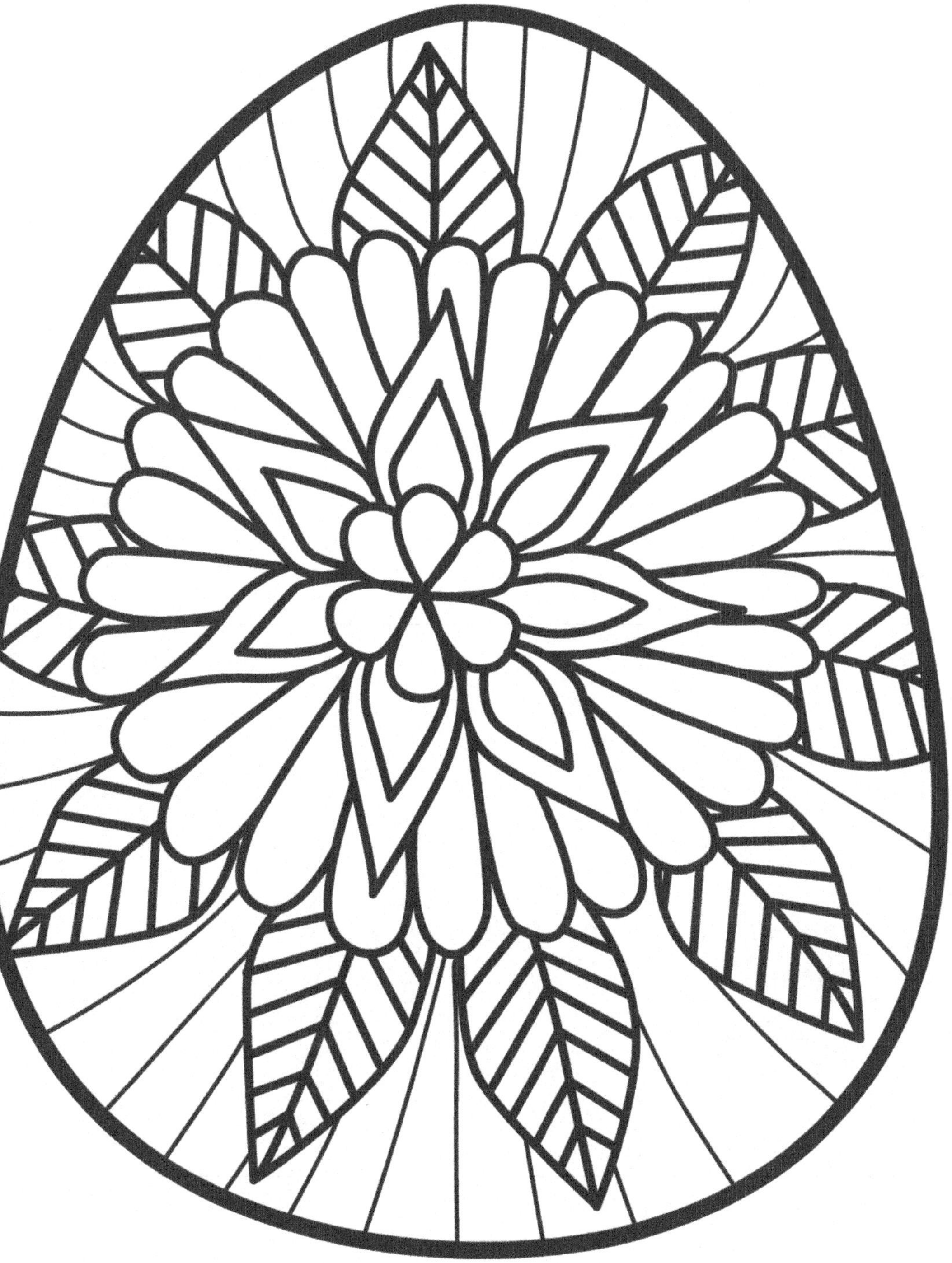

Made in the USA
Columbia, SC
21 March 2020

89787271R00046